TRACKS

AN ANIMAL TRACKING BOOK FOR KIDS

by Ann Schaefer, Ryan Schaefer,
John Schaefer, & Tina Howell

Printed in the United States of America

Print ISBN: 9780578721866
E-Book ISBN: 9780578721873

Canoe Tree Press

4697 Main Street
Manchester Center, VT 05255
Canoe Tree Press is a division of DartFrog Books.

 # Table of Contents

🐾 Let's Have An Adventure!!

Have you gone camping and discovered in the morning that you had a visitor while you were sleeping? Have you gone out to the woods and seen a fleeting glimpse of a critter only to find it left a few signs of some of its activities? After a fresh snow have you run into your backyard to discover you weren't the first one to make tracks?

It's time to become forensic animal detectives!

Did you know the average bald eagle nest is 4-5 feet in diameter and 2-4 feet deep? Each year the adult pair will add 1-2 feet of new material to the nest. The largest recorded bald eagle nest located in St. Petersburg Florida was 9.5 feet in diameter, 20 feet deep and weighed almost 3 tons!

Did you know that animals leave signs that help tell who they were and what they have been up to? By learning to identify these signs you can recognize what animal left them and get a little glimpse into their lives.

Animal tracks are left everywhere around you. Next time you go out your door look for these animal tracks. These can tell you if they are walking, feeding, pursuing prey, or evading predators. Sometimes these signs can even tell you if the animal was male or female. Additional signs, like chewed beaver logs, rotten insect logs, scat, rubs and wallows can tell you how they live and what they feed on.

There are some important tools you will need to help you examine animal tracks. The most important is something to measure with either a tape measure or a ruler. **We have included a ruler on the last page of this book.** Many animal tracks, like the deer and the elk, look very similar and the difference between the animal tracks is simply the size of the track. And to determine if an animal was walking, trotting or on the run it is best to have a tape measure to look at the distance between the tracks.

In this book we will teach you how to identify the animal tracks. You can keep track of the different animal tracks or signs that you have discovered and keep a record of where and when you found these signs. You can have an adult initial when you have identified each track.

So grab a tape measure, ask your parent's permission and lets head outside!

🐾 Measurements and Strides

Let's learn a little animal anatomy or parts of the animal's body, to help speak the animal language.

The toes of all animals are numbered from the inside of the foot, closest to the middle of the animal, to the outside of the animal. If you look at the back of your own hand, your thumb is #1 and your pinky finger is #5. In birds, toe #1 is not always present but when it is, it points backwards. In birds, toe #5 is absent. With amphibians, toe # 1 is absent on their front foot but remains on their hind foot. Alligators show all 5 toes in their front track, yet only 4 toes in their hind track.

Not all animals have large #1 toes: some do not have these toes at all, and in others the toe may be very small and higher up on the animal's leg like a dog. This high, small toe #1 is called a **dew claw**, shown in the diagram.

In deer, elk and sheep and other **ungulates** (hoofed animals) toe #1 is absent and toes #2 and #5 are smaller and are called the **dew claws.**

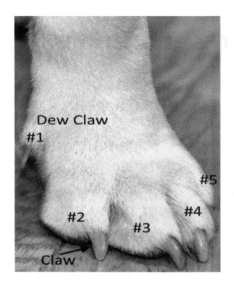

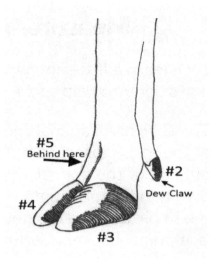

When measuring the track, you need to measure the minimum outline, the floor of the track. This will give more accurate information and help with identification.

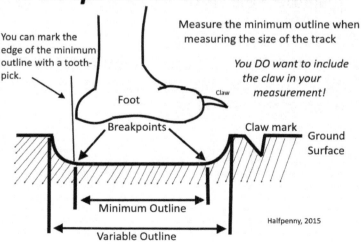

Footprint Cross-section

You can mark the edge of the minimum outline with a tooth-pick.

Measure the minimum outline when measuring the size of the track

You DO want to include the claw in your measurement!

Foot

Claw

Breakpoints

Claw mark

Ground Surface

Minimum Outline

Variable Outline

Halfpenny, 2015

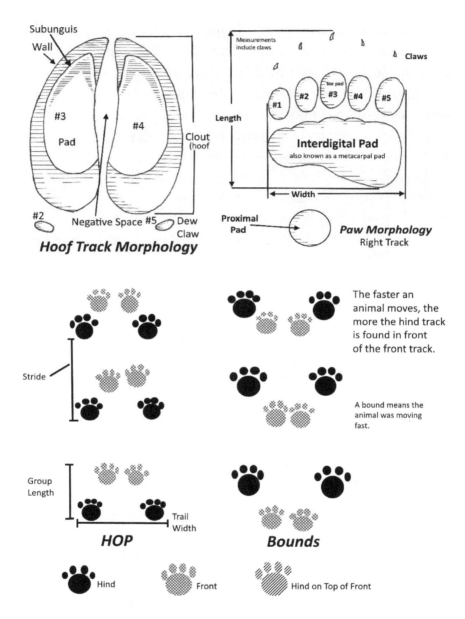

Hoof Track Morphology

Paw Morphology
Right Track

The faster an animal moves, the more the hind track is found in front of the front track.

A bound means the animal was moving fast.

HOP

Bounds

Hind

Front

Hind on Top of Front

Measuring strides can give a great deal of information. Trots, a gait in which evenly spaced footprints alternate on right and left sides of the line of travel, can indicate when a badger is actively hunting. Different kinds of strides are hops, bounds, lopes, gallops, **pronks** (like a deer jumping with all four legs at one time), walks, and skips. Various interpretations can be made from looking at these strides. These interpretations differ in different habitats and are not always exact.

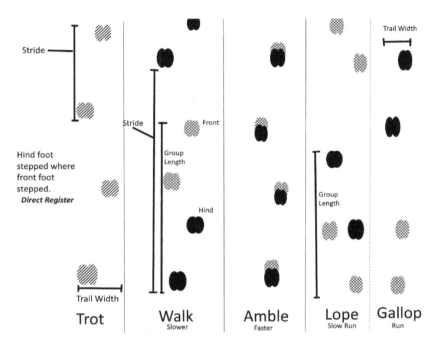

A **walk** is a slow gait in which each foot moves independently. At no point during the walking cycle with four feet, does the animal loose contact with the ground. A **direct register** track is where a hind foot lands on top of where the front foot stepped. If the hind footsteps beyond where the front foot had been, this is called an **overstep.** When an animal, such as a cat, **stalks**, it moves only one foot at a time cautiously and slowly. When a stalking animal moves the right rear foot forward and steps, then the right front moves and steps down; then the left rear followed by the left front. The trail is a track that results with the rear tracks pairing up with the front tracks, called an **understep walk.** With this understep walk, the hind track is found behind the front track (Elbroch, 2003).

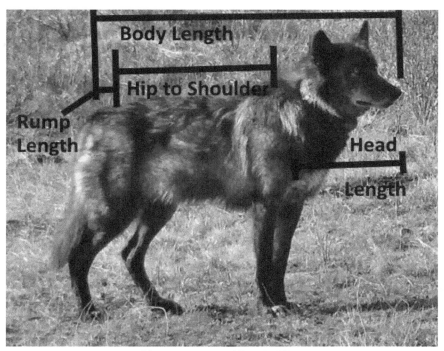

Photo courtesy of Troy LaFleur

A walking gait can help interpret the animal's size. With a normal walking gait pattern, the stride is 1 to 1.25 times longer than the distance from the hip to the shoulder of the animal. An estimated head length and rump length needs to be added to this length, the sum of which will then give us an estimate for the size of the animal.

Speed can also affect a gait pattern in a trail. Three rules of animal physiology demonstrate how speed can change the trail pattern.

As speed increases, the hind foot lands farther forward than the front track on the same side. As speed decreases, the hind foot lands farther back in relation to the front track.

As the speed of the animal increases, the track stride length increases.

As the speed of the animal increases, the straddle or width of the track group decreases. (Halfpenny, 2015)

Some possible interpretation examples includes the following: For a coyote the under-step walk can mean extreme rest, while an overstep walk can mean exploration. The direct register walk can mean hunting. The extended direct register walk can mean they are excited. The slow lope can mean play and communication. The coyote lope can mean discomfort or fear. The coyote bound can mean alarm or fear. The coyote gallop can mean fear. Different animal strides will have different meanings.

Measuring strides can help us identify the animal. It is important to measure the floor of the track and not the walls or drag marks. Make sure to measure the claw or nail marks but not the dew claws from hoofed animals. Trots and walks are measured from the tip of the front track to the tip of the next front track. A trail width known as **straddle** is taken from their widest points. Measuring the trails can help with identification of an animal when it is too difficult to identify the animal from the track alone

At times it is difficult to locate an entire stride. There is still information, however, that can be gathered from single tracks. For example, if the dirt is disturbed toward the toe of a hoofed animal such an elk, this means the elk is loping or galloping. Additionally, especially if you are hunting, looking at the track in the snow and seeing if there are crystals on the outside edge is one of the only ways to tell how old a track is. If the crystals are there, then the track is older. It can also be important to note specific events, such as the last time it rained. Checking to see if a track if has been disturbed by rain (looks like edges have melted), can help you determine the age of a track.

 Creating Your Own Tracking Plate
(Bring the Tracks to You!!)

You can create your own track plate to get animals to leave tracks giving you some additional practice at identifying the tracks. You will need some supplies:

Supplies:

- A large box
- Rubbing alcohol
- Tape
- A medium paintbrush
- A bowl
- Contact paper
- A cutting utensil or scissors
- Some sort of bait like peanut butter
- Powdered chalk. (I like straight line chalk that is used for straight line strings in construction, this can usually be found at hardware stores.)

First cut off one end of the box. The size of the animal you will get can depend on the size of your box. When I am trying to get some larger animals, I will cut off one side and the top.

Place a thick strip of contact paper toward the opening of your box, sticky side down. Then use another piece of contact paper with the sticky side up to line the rest of the bottom of your box. I usually use 4 pieces of tape to help affix this contact paper to the floor of the box.

Next, in a bowl mix rubbing alcohol and chalk until you have a thin paste. The amounts of alcohol and chalk in the end will really not matter. You want this runny enough to be able to paint a consistent coat of paste on your contact paper that has the sticky side down. Paint the contact paper that is closer to the opening all the way to the sides of the box. When the alcohol evaporates this leaves a perfect layer of chalk for the animal to walk through. Then when the animal steps on the sticky contact paper it will leave a perfect chalk track.

Don't forget the bait: smear some peanut butter on the rear wall of your box. Leave the box outside on level ground and check back the next day. The best placement would be on a well-used animal trail.

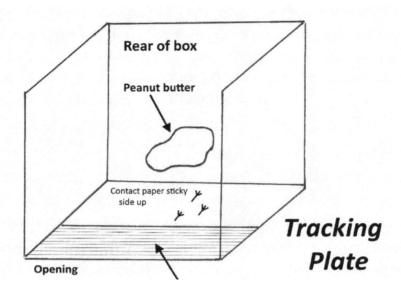

Rear of box

Peanut butter

Contact paper sticky side up

Opening

Tracking Plate

It can take a couple attempts or multiple tracking plates to get an animal to leave its marks. Keep in mind, if it rains, the contact paper will no longer be sticky and will need to be replaced. After a day, check your tracking plate for tracks. You can carefully peel up the tracked paper and place plain paper on it. Then when you turn it over you have secured your tracks for identification.

 Plaster Casting Tracks

Another fun way to help you examine your tracks is to create a plaster cast. When I have difficulty identifying a track, I find that if I can make a cast, it can show wonderful detail and preserve this evidence

The supplies you will need are:

- Plaster of Paris (this can be picked up at hardware stores, do not get Polyplaster or plaster for wallboard or patching compound; these do not get hard enough to preserve a cast.)
- A container to carry a portion in. Two pounds of plaster powder can make multiple casts.
- A flexible plastic cup, for example a medium size soda cup.
- A bottle of water will be needed if no water source is available
- A heavy duty spatula or spoon will be needed for mixing.

I keep a backpack loaded with these supplies when I head out for tracking.

1. Find some tracks you want to cast. Pick out one or two of the best ones.
2. When you find a track you want to cast, take some mud, sticks or stones and dirt and build a small circular wall around your track to contain

the plaster when it is poured. Make the wall ¼ to ½ an inch thick if possible. It is important to have your cast fairly thick or it is more fragile

3. Fill your cup 1/3 of water. To mix the plaster it needs to be mixed 2/3 plaster to 1/3 water.
4. Slowly sprinkle plaster into your cup while constantly mixing. Use your spatula to occasionally scrape the sides. You want to mix quickly because it can begin to set up. The consistency of thick pancake batter is desired.
5. Hold your spatula close to the track and pour the plaster down the spatula onto the track. Pour into the fine detailed areas of the track then into the rest of the track. Pour the track until it fills the mud retaining wall.
6. Gently vibrate the spatula shallowly in the plaster that is poured into the track to work out any bubbles.
7. Allow the plaster to dry for 30 minutes.
8. Gently use your fingers to dig out the mud retaining wall and pry up your cast.
9. Wash off some of the dirt under flowing water to rinse off the dirt. Only wash using your fingers, do not scrub, this can cause the plaster to crumble and break off details. Leave some of the dirt, it is a great highlighter to show off details.
10. Let the cast cure for several days to completely harden. If you need to transport, do not wrap in plastic, it traps in moisture and can cause the plaster to break.

Taking out the cast from the track usually destroys the original track. It is important to take a container like a bag to pick up every drop of plaster that has dried or dripped and leave not trace. Other materials or techniques are needed for casting tracks in snow.

🐾 Scat and Track Identification Games

Match the Scat!

Rabbit

Bison

Bobcat

Goose

Turkey

Raccoon

Moose

How Many Can You Identify?

Turkey	Green Sea Turtle	Black Bear
Raccoon	Snowshoe Hare	Alligator
Opossum	Porcupine	Mountain Goat
Bison	Striped Skunk	Goose
Bobcat	Beaver	Otter

TRACKS

1._____   10._____

2._____   11._____

3._____   12._____

4._____   13._____

5._____   14._____

6._____   15._____

7._____   16._____

8._____   17._____

9._____   18._____

Seek and Find

Can You find: Toad Hind Track, Mountain Goat Track, Pheasant, Great Blue Heron, Hooded Skunk Hind Track, Bighorn Sheep Track, Grizzly bear front track, Cottontail rabbit hind tracks.

Can You Name Animal Groups?

Bears:_____ Raccoon: _____
Wolves:_____ Badger: _____
Coyote: _____ Opossum: _____
Fox: _____ Prairie Dog: _____
Bighorn sheep: _____ Squirrel: _____
Mountain Goat: _____ Cougar:_____
Bison:_____ Bobcat: _____
Moose: _____ Alligator: _____
Caribou: _____ Turtle: _____
Pronghorn antelope:_____ Bullfrog: _____
Deer: _____ Toad:_____
Elk: _____ Rattlesnake:_____
Wild boar: _____ Turkey: _____
Snoeshoe hare:_____ Pheasant:_____
Mountain Cottontail: _____ Pelican: _____
Pika: _____ Quail: _____
Beaver: _____ Chipmunk: _____
Striped skunk:_____ Mallard duck: _____
Porcupine:_____ Goose:_____
River otter: _____ Heron:_____

 Bears

Ursus arctos and Ursus americanus

There are many different kinds of bears. We will specifically look at two bears that live in the United States; the black bear (Ursus americanus) and the grizzly bear (Ursus arctos, called a brown bear outside of North America)

Black Bear Territory
IUCN Red List (2019)

Grizzly Bear Territory
IUCN Red List (2019)

There are many differences between the black bear and the grizzly bear. The first and most obvious is the size. The black bear is much smaller than the grizzly bear. The grizzly bear boar (adult male) can weigh between 300 and 1,200 pounds and grow up to 9 feet in height. Black bear boars can weigh up to 550 pounds and grow up to 4 ½ feet in height. They actually come in many colors including, black, brown, blonde and cinnamon. In addition to their size difference the grizzly bear also has a large shoulder hump.

Ursus arctos

Notice the large shoulder hump of this blonde grizzly bear. Now compare it to the black bear without a shoulder hump and her cinnamon colored cub.

Ursus americanus

Black bears frequently have different habitat than grizzly bears, though there are also instances where their habitats overlap. Black bears prefer forest areas with a variety of fruit and nut-producing trees. One reason is these bears are very adept at climbing trees. Many times a mother bear will have her young climb a tree to keep them safe from danger. Black bear boars have been known to kill cubs in order to get the sow to want to mate again. Trees with a diameter larger than 20 inches around with strong furrowed bark are easily climbed. Black bears are very adaptable to different habitats. They can occupy hot dry shrubby forests of Mexico, mossy coniferous rainforests of coastal Alaska, steamy hardwood Cyprus swamps in Florida, and the treeless tundra of Labrador. They also prefer old growth trees for denning sites.

Grizzly bears prefer more open areas. They have been more known for their fishing skills during the summer, especially when the salmon are spawning. In early spring, when fruits have yet to ripen, grizzly bears have become specialized in habitats where specific types of prey are available. In Denali National Park, grizzlies have been seen hunting prairie dogs. They will rear up on their back legs and fall with their front paws close to a prairie dog hole, look around frantically to see what exit hole a prairie dog will pop out of, then run after it. One sign to look for are bear tracks around prairie dog holes. If this method doesn't work, their claws are longer than the black bear and more adept at digging the prairie dog up. In Yellowstone National Park, where the elk are plentiful, the grizzly bears are able to smell and detect where the new elk calves have been born. They find the calves easy prey. One cow elk decided to give birth in the middle of Mammoth Campground. She cleaned up all signs of the birth and lead her calf off. The next day a herd of park rangers was seen running to one end of the campground in a defensive charge protecting campers, and moments later, a grizzly was charging back out of the campground where the elk had calved. Grizzly bears can live above the tree line up to elevations of 16,000 feet. Their muscular shoulder hump and hefty claws make them better adapted to digging up small animals, insects and roots. Their more robust jaw muscles enable them to process more fibrous food like roots. They also enjoy the thick temperate rainforests of coastal British Columbia and Alaska.

Black bears are usually **nocturnal** (active at night); however **sows** (mothers with cubs), will come out during the day with their cubs because they know that the **boars** (adult males) are sleeping. Sows with cubs are more likely to be seen during dawn and dusk. There are twice as many black bears living than there are all other types of bears added together.

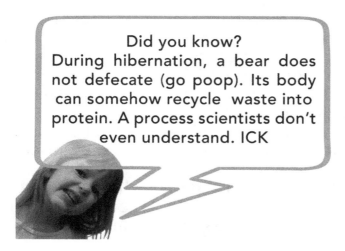

Did you know?
During hibernation, a bear does not defecate (go poop). Its body can somehow recycle waste into protein. A process scientists don't even understand. ICK

Bears are **omnivores,** which means they eat both plant material and animal material. One of the signs they leave behind that tells you what they have been eating is their poop or scat. In early spring when they first come out of hibernation you will notice that their scat has hair in it. This shows they have been eating meat. In the summer, when berries are full grown and likely to be ripe, their scat is less formed and seeds can be usually seen.

This bear has been eating animals, notice the fur

This bear has been eating berries, notice the seeds.

In early spring, another sign to look for is areas of moss on the ground that have been rolled back. This is a sign that bears are hunting for bugs. Old rotten logs that have been clawed at or rolled over can be another sign of bears searching for a bug snack.

A bear has been digging for insects in this rotting log. Notice the small sticks and bits on top of the log. A bear will kick up these small parts when digging for bugs, normally a rotting log, the larger pieces fall to the ground.

There is a significant size difference between grizzly bears hind tracks, up to 14 inches long and 8 ½ inches wide, and black bears with the hind track between 6 and 9 inches long and 3 ¼ to 6 inches wide (Elbroch, 2003). Both bears have oval toes with the large toe on the outside of the paw in contrast to the human foot, where the "big" toe is larger than the other toes. The bear first toe is generally slightly smaller or doesn't always make the print. The hind foot track is long and human-like. The front paw is much shorter, with a shortened pad but oval toes that are similar in size. Grizzly bears generally have much longer claw marks than black bears. The claws are longer on the front paw than on the rear paw. Black bears also have more fur on their paws and they can be more obscured than the grizzly bear.

The black bear walking stride measures 17 to 25 inches in length and 8 to 14 inches in width. Their trot measures between 27 and 37 inches in length and 6 to 10 inches in width. Their lope measures 25 to 30 inches long (Elbroch, 2003).

The following photo and sketch are both right tracks:

Black Bear Front Track

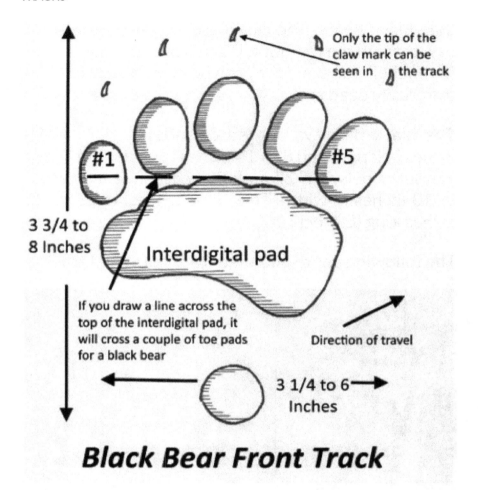

Black Bear Front Track

Toe #1 does not always show as seen in the track above. Toe # 5 is the largest. The interdigital pad has the smaller part of the wedge toward the center of the bear's body.

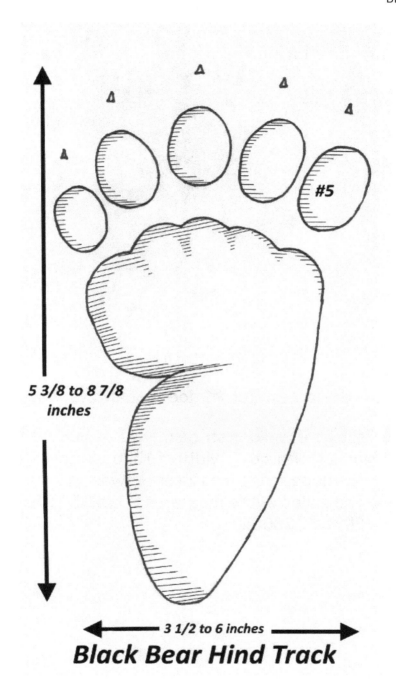

5 3/8 to 8 7/8 inches

#5

3 1/2 to 6 inches

Black Bear Hind Track

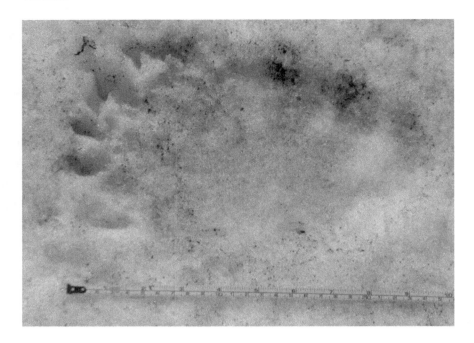

Grizzly Bear Hind Track

Toe #5 is the largest, Toe #1 does not always show.

The grizzly bear walking stride measures between 19 and 29 inches with a trail width of 13 to 20 inches. The grizzly bear lope stride measures between 18 and 33 inches. The gallop stride measures 30 to 35 inches in length (Elbroch, 2003).

8 1/4 to 14 Inches

Grizzly Bear Hind Track

#5

Toes are closer together than in other species. Has webbing between toes that can show up in tracks.

Direction of Travel

4 5/8 to 8 1/2 Inches

Toe #5 is the outside of the foot. This is a sketch of a hind right foot. Bears walk pigeon toed, toes pointed toward the center of their body

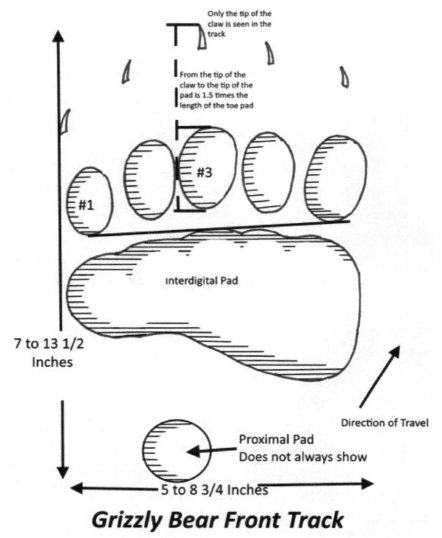

Only the tip of the claw is seen in the track

From the tip of the claw to the tip of the pad is 1.5 times the length of the toe pad

#3

#1

Interdigital Pad

7 to 13 1/2 Inches

Direction of Travel

Proximal Pad
Does not always show

5 to 8 3/4 Inches

Grizzly Bear Front Track

Unlike a black bear front track, when you draw a straight line over the top of the interdigital pad on a grizzly bear front track, the linxe does not cross the toes.

Personal Tracking Record:

Front Track ☐   Hind Track ☐   Scat ☐

Other Sign Found: _____

Date Found: _____

Habitat Found: _____

Place Found: _____

Parent's Initials: _____

Personal Tracking Record:

Front Track ☐   Hind Track ☐   Scat ☐

Other Sign Found: _____

Date Found: _____

Habitat Found: _____

Place Found: _____

Parent's Initials: _____

Personal Tracking Record:

Front Track ☐   Hind Track ☐   Scat ☐

Other Sign Found: _____

Date Found: _____

Habitat Found: _____

Place Found: _____

Parent's Initials: _____

Wolves

Canis lupus

Wolves Territory
IUCN Red List (2019)

Wolves are pack animals. The **alpha pair**, the leaders, mate for life. They have a litter of pups every year averaging five to six pups. The litter size can increase with a greater amount of food available in their territory. The basic family unit includes the alpha pair, three to six juveniles (younger than 1 year old), and one to three yearlings (between 1 and 2 years old). There can be one to three family units in a pack. Once the pups are born they will stay with the pack from 10 months to 4 ½ years. Pups will break off from the pack when they are old enough to mate or there is too much competition for food.

They have very specialized fur. They have fluffy dense winter fur with short underfur and long coarse guard hair. They can rest comfortably in the open in temperatures down to 40 degrees below zero by curling up and placing their muzzles (snouts) between their hind legs and covering their faces with their tails. This fur does not collect ice when warm air is breathed on it. Most of these guard hairs and the underfur are shed during the spring and grows back during the fall.

Wolves will set up very specific territories that are mainly for hunting food. They will increase this territory if their food supply decreases inside their current territory. They will also increase their territory when their pups reach 6 months old or need the same amount of food as adults. They tend not to hunt on the edges of their territory to avoid encountering neighbor wolf packs. Wolves will defend their territory from other wolf packs with a combination of scent marking by urination (peeing), leaving scat and ground scratches, howling, and directly attacking other packs. Scent marks, potty spots, are left every 240 meters throughout their territory on regular travel ways and junctions. These markers last two to three weeks and are left near rocks or boulders, trees, and skeletons of large animals. These territorial fights with other packs are the primary cause of death among wolves.

Their hunt has five stages: locating the prey, the stalk, the encounter, the rush, and the chase.

Wolves eat a wide range of foods. Most of their food is from killing animals larger than themselves such as moose, elk, deer, sheep, goats, caribou, musk oxen and bison. They are pack hunters that are able to take down these larger animals because they work together. Voles, beaver and hares add to their diet as well as berries and some carrion, dead decaying meat. Because of pack hunting there can be many tracks from multiple animals together. This can make it a little confusing to identify exactly how many wolves are leaving the tracks.

Gray Wolf Hind Track

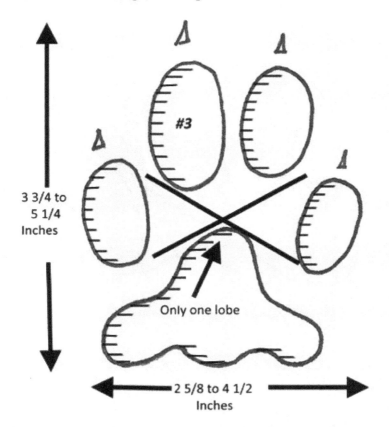

3 3/4 to
5 1/4
Inches

#3

Only one lobe

2 5/8 to 4 1/2
Inches

Gray Wolf Front Track

Direction of
Travel

3

3 3/4 to 5 3/4
Inches

Only one lobe

2 7/8 to 5
Inches

Wolf front paw tracks are larger than their hind foot tracks. On the primary pad toward the toes there is only one lobe, though this is fused with the hind two pads into one making it appear triangular shaped. The negative space between the pads forms an X. The front tracks measure between 3 ¾ and 5 ¾ inches long, and 2 7/8 to 5 inches wide. The hind track measures 3 ¾ inches to 5 ¼ inches wide (Elbroch, 2003). This is very distinctive from cats, which have two lobes at the front of the main pad. The primary difference when distinguishing between wolves and other dogs or canines is the size. One additional difference when looking at wolves and cats is that a wolf track will include claw marks.

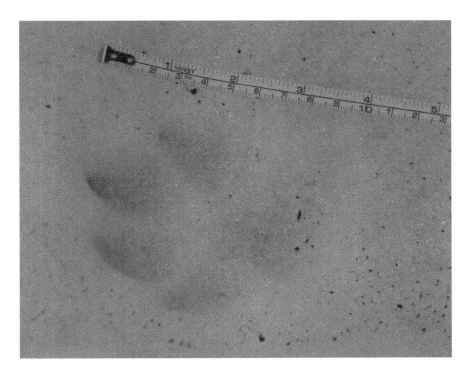

The wolf walking stride measures from 13 to 24 inches in length with a trail width between 6 and 10 inches wide. The lope stride measures from 20 to 23 inches in length. The wolf gallop stride measures from 6 to 68 inches in length. The wolf direct register trot stride measures from 22 to 34 inches in length with a trail width between 4 and 9 ¼ inches wide (Elbroch, 2003).

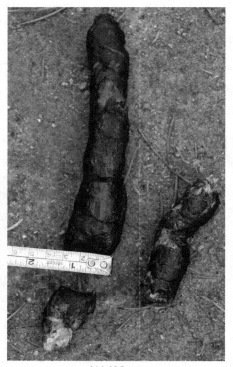

Wolf Scat

When evaluating a wolf trail, you can determine if the wolf is a male or female when you come upon a urine mark. If the mark is in the middle of the trail and both back tracks are present it is a female. If the urine mark is off to the side with the hind leg in the middle of the trail then it is likely to be a male. However, some alpha females will lift their leg to mark territories so it is important to evaluate if the urine mark is next to the hind leg track or behind the hind track.

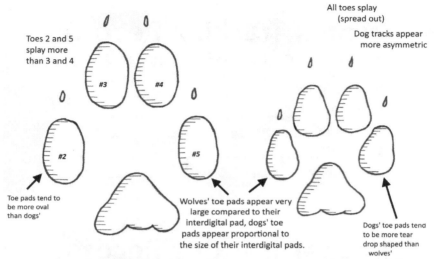

All toes splay (spread out)

Dog tracks appear more asymmetric

Toes 2 and 5 splay more than 3 and 4

#3 #4

#2

#5

Toe pads tend to be more oval than dogs'

Wolves' toe pads appear very large compared to their interdigital pad, dogs' toe pads appear proportional to the size of their interdigital pads.

Dogs' toe pads tend to be more tear drop shaped than wolves'

Wolf Track   *Dog Track*

Differences Between Wolf and Dog Tracks

It is impossible to differentiate 100% between wolf tracks and dog tracks with certainty!! There are, however, subtle differences to look for. The most obvious difference is the size. Wolf tracks average 4 inches in both length and width. Dog tracks average less than 4 inches. There are some species of large dogs whose tracks do measure greater than 4 inches. Wolf internal toe pads of toes #3 and 4 sit more forward of the **lateral** (outside) toes of #2 and #5. Wolf lateral toes are the toes that splay while a dog's toes all splay evenly. Dog toe pads tend to be more teardrop shaped than wolf toe pads. The toe pads of the wolf appear very large compared to their interdigital pad. Lastly, dog tracks overall appear asymmetrical compared to the wolf track.

Personal Tracking Record:

Front Track ☐   Hind Track ☐   Scat ☐

Other Sign Found: _____

Date Found: _____

Habitat Found: _____

Place Found: _____

Parent's Initials: _____

Personal Tracking Record:

Front Track ☐   Hind Track ☐   Scat ☐

Other Sign Found: _____

Date Found: _____

Habitat Found: _____

Place Found: _____

Parent's Initials: _____

Personal Tracking Record:

Front Track ☐   Hind Track ☐   Scat ☐

Other Sign Found: _____

Date Found: _____

Habitat Found: _____

Place Found: _____

Parent's Initials: _____

Coyote

Canis latrans

The coyote's size varies depending on where they live. They are larger in most of North America, and smaller in Mexico and Central America. Coyotes in higher elevations tend to be more black and gray, while the more desert coyotes tend to be red and whitish gray.

Coyote Territory
IUCN Red List (2019)

Along with the color of their fur, the density of their fur also varies from North America to Central America. In the United States and Canada, the coyotes fur is longer and denser, while the Mexican and Central American coyote's fur is almost bristly. The coyote is a medium-size canine with a narrow muzzle, large pointed ears, and long slender legs that help them run up to 40 miles per hour. They are primarily light gray or red in color mixed with black and white. They also live up to 14 1/2 years.

Coyotes may live alone or in packs. They are highly adaptable and can live from the Arctic tundra to the inner city of Los Angeles. While most predators ranges are shrinking, the coyote's range is increasing. As well as being adaptable to where they live, they are also adaptable to what they eat. Coyotes usually hunt small prey by themselves but two or more coyotes will hunt prey larger than they are. Coyotes are opportunistic predators. They are even known to have a **symbiotic relationship** (a close relationship between two species in which at least one species benefits) and even friendships with badgers while hunting. The coyote will wait by the exit hole while the badger goes after the prey down the primary hole in order to catch the prey sneaking out their back door. Coyotes have been seen to even rest their muzzles on the head of the badger and have the badger tolerate the coyote licking their face. To see more how badgers and coyotes work together see our chapter on badgers.

Did you know?
Coyotes can climb trees!
If a coyote thinks it can get a meal, it will pursue prey up a tree.

Coyotes may eat anything from fruit and insects to mice and antelope. They will even fish or climb trees to find food. This makes a very wide variety of areas where coyote tracks can be found. Scientist have shown that the coyote relies more on its vision for hunting than it does smell or sound.

A pack of coyotes yipping to each other to coordinate a hunt.

Coyotes are **monogamous**, only having one mate. The female will attract mates by scent marking and increased howling. When she has attracted a number of males, she will pick her mate, then they will set up a territory, and either make their own den or take over an abandoned hole. During the female's pregnancy, the male hunts alone and the female will stay in the den with dried grass and fur she has pulled off of her belly. She will scratch and continuously clean out the den until the pups are born.

Females will have one litter of pups a year averaging 6 pups. They are born blind but at 3 weeks begin to eat semi-solid food that is vomited up by both parents and the pack members. (I bet you are appreciating your mother's cooking right about now.) Most young disperse in the first year and travel up to 10 miles to settle down. Pack life includes social bonding, raising pups, and territory defense. The alpha pair are the only coyotes to breed. Juveniles from previous litters help look after the younger puppies.

Coyotes are much smaller in size than wolves. Coyotes are between 28 and 38 inches in length and weigh from 17 pounds to 48 pounds. Coyote tracks are very similar to wolf tracks, but size is the largest difference. Coyote tracks are 2 to 3 inches long compared with wolf tracks that are 5 to 6 inches long. The coyote's front track measures 2 ¼ to 3 ½ inches in length and 1 ½ to 2 7/8 inches wide (Elbroch, 2003).

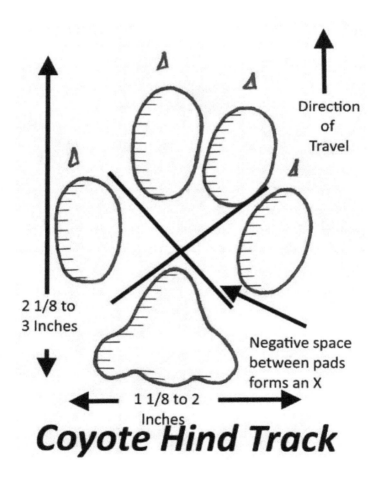

Direction of Travel

2 1/8 to 3 Inches

Negative space between pads forms an X

1 1/8 to 2 Inches

Coyote Hind Track

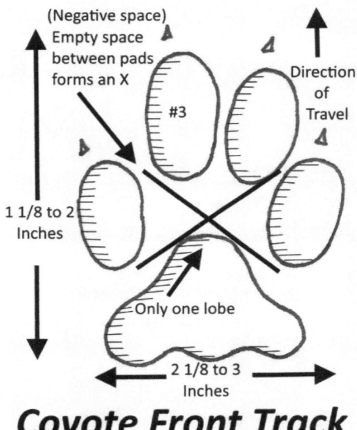

(Negative space)
Empty space
between pads
forms an X

Direction
of
Travel

#3

1 1/8 to 2
Inches

Only one lobe

2 1/8 to 3
Inches

Coyote Front Track

Four toes usually show in the tracks. The hind pad is fused, showing a triangle shape. The negative space between the pads forms an X. The coyote tracks are also similar to fox tracks but are wider. They also will usually show claw marks.

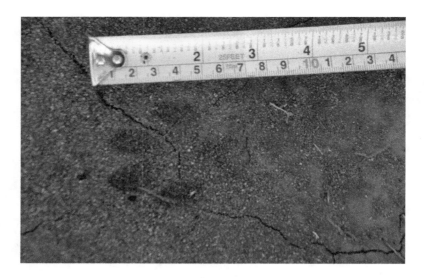

Coyote scat will have fur in it and occasional vegetation. It will turn white after a short period.

Coyote Scat

Personal Tracking Record:

Front Track ☐   Hind Track ☐   Scat ☐

Other Sign Found: _____

Date Found: _____

Habitat Found: _____

Place Found: _____

Parent's Initials: _____

Personal Tracking Record:

Front Track ☐   Hind Track ☐   Scat ☐

Other Sign Found: _____

Date Found: _____

Habitat Found: _____

Place Found: _____

Parent's Initials: _____

Personal Tracking Record:

Front Track ☐   Hind Track ☐   Scat ☐

Other Sign Found: _____

Date Found: _____

Habitat Found: _____

Place Found: _____

Parent's Initials: _____

 Red Fox

Vulpes vulpes

The red fox is a 3 foot long, 2 foot tall canine with a pale yellowish red to deep reddish brown coat with a white to ash underside. Their lower legs is usually black with a bushy tail that has a white or black tip. Mature fox have yellow eyes with a dark brown or black nose.

Of all carnivores, the red fox is one of the most widely spread throughout different regions of the world with different temperature ranges, and is the most adaptable. The red fox has even been found in colder areas than the arctic fox. They even live in city centers. The red fox can adapt to multiple habitats including forest, tundra, prairie, desert, mountains, farmlands and urban areas preferring mixed vegetation such as edge habitats and mixed scrub woodland.

Red Fox Territory
IUCN Red List (2019)

They are opportunistic foragers. The red fox is a solitary hunter. Their hunting techniques include stealth, pouncing, and dash-and-grab. When they catch mice, they will leap, springing 3 feet off the ground and diving paws first onto the prey. They use this same technique to dive into the snow to get rodents living under the blanket of snow. Their diet includes small mammals, rodents, birds, beetles, earthworms, fish and fruit when available. Part of why they can live in so many areas is because they are very adaptable about what they are willing to eat. The red fox has a great memory for where it has previously found food.

The red fox has binocular vision (using both eyes working together to create a three-dimensional image) and reacts mainly to seeing movement. They have very sensitive hearing. They can hear mice squeaking at 330 feet and can hear the low frequency sounds of rodents digging underground. They have a good sense of smell but is weaker than that of specialized dogs.

"Did you know? The red fox has partially retractable claws! Cats' claws are fully retractable. Crazy!"

The red fox has kits (babies) only one time a year, with the average litter between four and six kits. The kits are born in a burrow either dug by the vixen (female) or abandoned by other animals or in rock crevices. The kits are born blind, deaf, and toothless. The mothers remain with the kits for two to three weeks because the kits aren't able to regulate their body temperatures. During this time, the fathers will feed the vixen but will not enter the maternity den. The vixen is extremely protective and will fight dogs to protect their kits. If the mother dies before the kits are independent, the father will take over raising them. They are generally considered **monogamous**, father and mother will only mate with each other, but scientists have found some **communal denning** where multiple adults live in the same den. The kits will leave the den and experiment with solid food at three to four weeks. They are adult size when they reach six to seven months. They live about five years in the wild. Outside of the denning season, the red fox prefers to live in dense shrubby areas.

"Did you know? The fox will train their kits to eat solid food while weaning them, by regurgitating the food they have eaten to feed their kits to eat. Gross!"

Because the red fox has hairy feet, its tracks may be blurred in snow or in mud. The front tracks range from 1 7/8 inches long 2 7/8 inches and 1 3/8 to 2 1/8 inches wide. They have five toes but toe number one is smaller and raised up on the inner leg. Fox tracks are narrow compared to coyote tracks. The red fox walking stride measures 8 to 12 inches in length. The trot stride measures 13 to 20 inches in length and the trail width 2 to 3 ¾ inches. The fox lope stride measures 9 to 15 inches in length. The fox gallop stride measures 8 to 55 inches in length (Elbroch, 2003). Because of their diet, their scat may have fur or signs of berries, as shown here. The cherries were in season when this fox had his snack.

This fox has been eating the local cherries

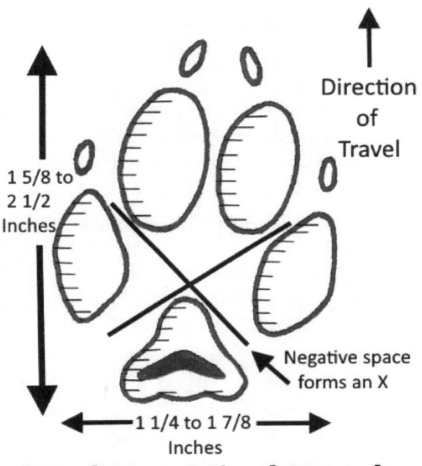

1 5/8 to 2 1/2 Inches

Direction of Travel

Negative space forms an X

1 1/4 to 1 7/8 Inches

Red Fox Hind Track

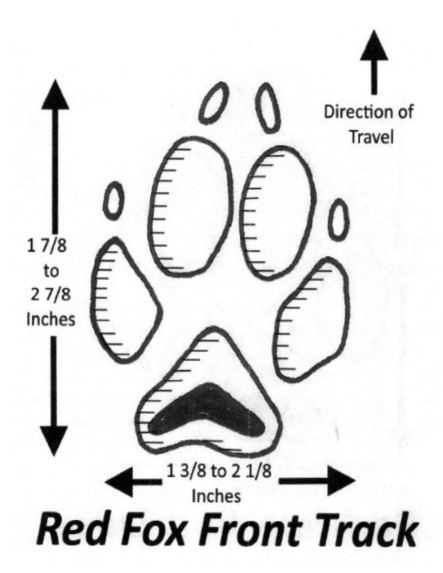

Direction of Travel

1 7/8 to 2 7/8 Inches

1 3/8 to 2 1/8 Inches

Red Fox Front Track

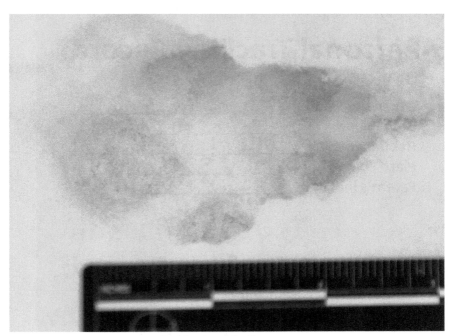

Red fox track in the snow

Personal Tracking Record:
Front Track ☐   Hind Track ☐   Scat ☐

Other Sign Found: _____
Date Found: _____
Habitat Found: _____
Place Found: _____
Parent's Initials: _____

Personal Tracking Record:
Front Track ☐   Hind Track ☐   Scat ☐

Other Sign Found: _____
Date Found: _____
Habitat Found: _____
Place Found: _____
Parent's Initials: _____

Personal Tracking Record:
Front Track ☐   Hind Track ☐   Scat ☐

Other Sign Found: _____
Date Found: _____
Habitat Found: _____
Place Found: _____
Parent's Initials: _____

 Bighorn Sheep

Ovis canadensis

Bighorn Sheep escape their predators by running and climbing. They inhabit open dry lands, alpine meadows, grassy mountain slopes and foothill country close to cliffs. They will browse quickly and eat large amounts of vegetation then return to the safety of the cliffs. Since bighorn sheep cannot move through deep snow, they prefer drier slopes where annual snowfall is less than about 60 inches per year. A bighorn's winter range usually is at lower elevations than its summer range. Bighorn sheep graze on grasses, herbs, sedges, ferns, mosses, lichens, twigs and leaves.

Bighorn Sheep Territory
IUCN Red List (2019)

Bighorns have massive curling horns but no chin beard. They have short tails and a large rump patch. They have wide set eyes that give them a wide angle of vision to see in front and to the sides. They also have a good sense of hearing and sensitive sense of smell aiding them in detecting predators from great distances. Additionally, bighorn sheep have special-ized hooves with rough pads that provide a natural grip allowing them to jump from ledge to ledge over

20 feet. Bighorn sheep can vary in size depending on the areas they inhabit. Bighorns from the Rocky Mountains can have the largest males, which can exceed 500 pounds, while females can exceed 200 pounds. Male bighorns from the Sierra Nevada's are smaller and but can weigh up to 200 pounds and females up to 140 pounds. Females, **ewes**, have horns but their horns are shorter and less curved. Bighorns come in various shades of brown, from light to gray-ish to dark chocolate. They have white rumps, and the backs of their legs are lined with white as well and white around their muzzle. Male bighorn sheep, **rams**, have large horn cores, as well as enlarged cornual and frontal sinuses (bone cavities that go from the horn and nose to the skull. These adaptations protect the brain by absorbing the impact when the males head butt as a form of fighting for dominance for females. Bighorn sheep have true horns that do not shed and will grow additional rings every year.

You can see here that the big horn ewe appears much different than the ram with her significantly smaller horns.

Bighorns live in large herds up to 100 but do not follow a single dominant ram. Prior to the **rut**, (the mating period), the rams challenge each other to determine mating access for ewes. During this pre-rut period, the rams will clash horns in competition. Two rams will walk away from each other, turn to face each other, then jump and lunge into headbutts. Bighorn rams have three different techniques for courting. One strategy is called "tending," where he will follow and defends a ewe that is ready to mate. A second strategy is to fight for a ewe that is already tended by another ram. Rams will also try a blocking strategy. They will prevent a ewe from accessing the tending areas before she goes into season and is ready to mate.

In the spring, when a ewe is ready to give birth, she will find a secluded cliff to have her lamb. Within a day the lamb is able to walk and climb. The white wooly lamb with short horns will stay on the secluded birthing area for 5 days before it will begin to follow it's mother around. Lambs are weaned around 5 months old. When the lambs are a few weeks old, they will form their own nursery herd within the group and only return to their mothers when nursing.

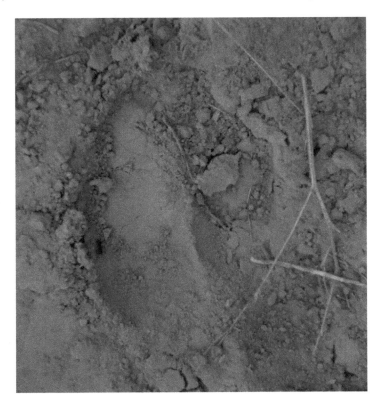

The bighorn's front track measures 2 1/8 to 3 3/8 inches in length. The width is 1 ½ to 3 inches wide. Their hooves are pointed and more heart shaped than those of the mountain goat. The front track is larger than the hind track. The Bighorn's hind track measures 2 1/16 to 3 ¼ inches long and 1 ½ to 2 3/8 inches wide. These measurements are similar to those of the mountain goat. The bighorn sheep's walking stride measures 12 to 25 inches in length and the trail width is 4 to 11 inches. Their trot stride measures 23 to 35 inches in length and 3 to 6 inches in width (Elbroch, 2003).

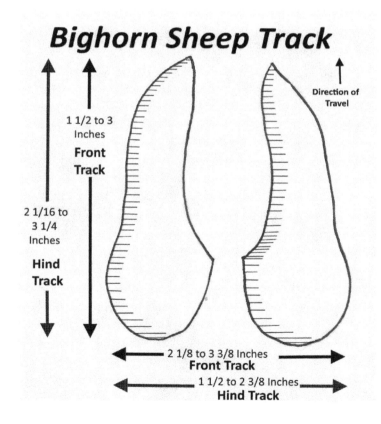

Bighorn Sheep Track

Direction of Travel

1 1/2 to 3 Inches

Front Track

2 1/16 to 3 1/4 Inches

Hind Track

2 1/8 to 3 3/8 Inches
Front Track

1 1/2 to 2 3/8 Inches
Hind Track

Personal Tracking Record:

Front Track ☐   Hind Track ☐   Scat ☐

Other Sign Found: _____

Date Found: _____

Habitat Found: _____

Place Found: _____

Parent's Initials: _____

Personal Tracking Record:

Front Track ☐   Hind Track ☐   Scat ☐

Other Sign Found: _____

Date Found: _____

Habitat Found: _____

Place Found: _____

Parent's Initials: _____

Personal Tracking Record:

Front Track ☐   Hind Track ☐   Scat ☐

Other Sign Found: _____

Date Found: _____

Habitat Found: _____

Place Found: _____

Parent's Initials: _____

 Mountain Goat

Oreamnos americanus

The mountain goat, also known as the Rocky Mountain goat, is a surefooted climber seen on cliffs and ice. Amazing climbers, they seem to be able to climb almost vertical walls of rock. The mountain goat has a hard keratinous sheath and a soft pad that allows them to gain traction on the smallest of granite cracks while simultaneously gripping maximum surface area. The male is known as a **billy** and the female is known as a **nanny.** Both the male and female have beards, short tails and long black horns. Their horns are 5.9 to 11 inches long and have yearly growth rings. They have true horns that do not shed like antlers. Mountain goats have wooly white double coats. There is a dense wool undercoat protected by an outer layer of longer hollow hair. They **molt,** (shed), their extra wool in spring by rubbing against rocks and trees, and the high wind also helps with molting. The mountain goat's wool coat can help them withstand temperatures as low as negative 50 degrees Fahrenheit and winds up to 100 miles per hour.

The billies are about 3.3 feet tall. Males weigh 30% more than the females. Mountain goats weigh between 99 and 309 pounds. Billies have longer horns and beards than the females.

Mountain Goat Territory
IUCN Red List (2019)

Mountain goats usually stay above the tree line throughout the year but will migrate seasonally to higher terrain in summer or lower elevations in winter. Mountain Goats are usually confined to areas on the same mountain face. Their daily movements depend on the goats needs for food, rest, security from predators, and keeping their temperature controlled. They migrate during the season due to need for food, to breed, and to have offspring.

Mountain goats are found more on the face of cliffs than bighorn sheep. They can tolerate the snow more than bighorn sheep and will be even seen on the coastal ranges of Alaska where they tolerate a higher level of humidity than bighorn sheep or dall sheep. They avoid predators by jumping among rocks and terrain through which predators are unable to maneuver. Mountain goats' hooves have a hard outer rim surrounding a rubbery inner surface, providing excellent traction.

Mountain goats live between 12 and 15 years. Their lifespan depends on how their teeth wear down. When preparing to mate, the billy will stare at the nanny for long periods and dig rutting pits that are between 25 to 50 mm deep. Billies will take dust baths in these ruts, bed down in them during the mid-day and night. Additionally, wallowing assists in shedding winter coats and possibly removing parasites. Because of wallowing in ruts, the billies tend to appear dirtier than females. Males may mark a female, "claim it," by rubbing a musky oil that is secreted from a gland at the base of their horns. Males rarely head butt when competing for mates. Their skulls and horns are more fragile than those of bighorn sheep. When fighting, billies stand side by side and stab at each other's flanks. They have thick skin in this area as protection. Regardless, there are deaths associated with stabbing wounds to the chest, neck or abdomen. Both males and females usually mate with multiple individuals during breeding season.

The newborn mountain goats are called **kids**. Kids are born on steep cliffs as a method of avoiding predators. They are able to scramble around on the rocks at only one day old following their mothers. They are weaned after about one month and live with their mother for about a year or until the nanny has the next offspring. Nannies protect the kids by leading them out of danger, standing over them when faced by a predator, and positioning themselves below their kids on steep slopes to stop their free falls. Nannies will fight over their space and food sources. They will also fight each other for dominance over the group. They will circle each other with their heads lowered displaying their horns.

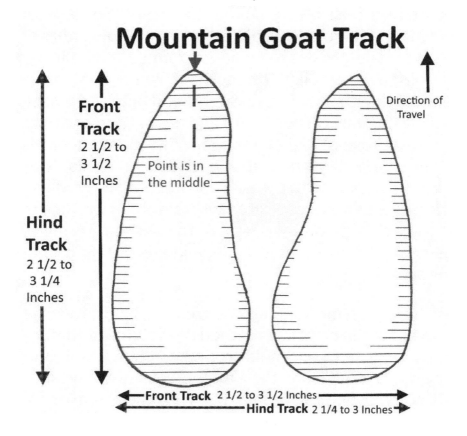

Mountain Goat Track

Front Track 2 1/2 to 3 1/2 Inches

Hind Track 2 1/2 to 3 1/4 Inches

Point is in the middle

Direction of Travel

←—**Front Track** 2 1/2 to 3 1/2 Inches—→
←—**Hind Track** 2 1/4 to 3 Inches→

The mountain goat's front track measures 2 ½ to 3 ½ inches in length and 2 ½ to 3 ½ inches in width. The hooves are pointed but the track shape is blocky. The sizes are similar to those of the bighorn sheep. The hind track measures 2 ½ to 3 ¼ inches in length and 2 ¼ to 3 inches in width. The mountain goat walking stride measures 15 to 30 inches in length and 8 to 13 inches in width (Elbroch, 2003).

Mountain Goat tracks are easily confused with Big Horn Sheep. Look for the point to be in the middle of the cleat. Additionally, mountain goat tracks are very blocky looking.

Personal Tracking Record:

Front Track ☐   Hind Track ☐   Scat ☐

Other Sign Found: _____

Date Found: _____

Habitat Found: _____

Place Found: _____

Parent's Initials: _____

Personal Tracking Record:

Front Track ☐   Hind Track ☐   Scat ☐

Other Sign Found: _____

Date Found: _____

Habitat Found: _____

Place Found: _____

Parent's Initials: _____

Personal Tracking Record:

Front Track ☐   Hind Track ☐   Scat ☐

Other Sign Found: _____

Date Found: _____

Habitat Found: _____

Place Found: _____

Parent's Initials: _____

 Bison

Bison bison

Wait a minute. That can't be right!

There, that's better.
That's the bison that left that scat.

Today Yellowstone National Park hosts the only unfenced free ranging-bison herd in the United States. Bison are highly social. They travel in herds. When not in breeding season, only the adult males will be found by themselves. During the **rut**, breeding season, adult males will fight for dominance. Only one in three males will breed. Females, called cows, will have a single calf in the spring.

Bison Territory
IUCN Red List (2019)

Bison are **nomadic**, always moving, grazing from field to field eating grasses and **sedges** (a grasslike plant with triangular stems, growing typically in wet ground).. They migrate to higher elevation grasslands during the summer and to lower range lands in the winter. Frequently when migrating, they can be seen traveling in lines. Because they keep these prairies healthy with their grazing and by fertilizing with their feces, scat, they are considered a key stone species. A **keystone species** has a role within the ecosystem that has an effect on the other organisms within the system, keeping their population numbers in balance. Other animals could not survive without the healthy prairie. The grazed prairies are shown to have 36-85% higher production of grass than un-grazed prairie. The high mineral content in the bison urine and feces helps with the fertilization. When snow is deep and prairie grasses are covered the bison will feed on sage brush.

Two helpful volunteers examining what the buffalo have been eating.

The bison are the largest living land animal in North America. Bison are 6 ½ to 11 ½ feet in length with a shoulder height between 60 and 73 inches. They can weigh between 700 and 2,205 pounds. The bison has a shaggy long dark brown coat in the winter and a lighter weight lighter brown coat in the summer. They have a distinctive shoulder hump and a huge head. Their hair is longer on the front half of their body. Both males and females have short curved horns that can grow up to 2 feet long. They will use these horns for fighting status within the herd and for defense. Bison can jump up to 6 feet and run from 35 to 40 miles per hour.

Bison calves are born with reddish-brown fur

The bison lives in river valleys, prairies and plains. Their typical habitat is open or semi-open grasslands, sagebrush, semiarid lands and scrublands. They graze on hilly or mountainous areas where the slopes are not too steep. The migration of the herds can be based on direction or on altitude. Bison have daily movements between foraging sites.

Bison will roll in a **wallow,** either wet or dry, to help shed their winter coat, get rid of insects, for **thermo-regulation**, keeping their temperature regulated, play behavior, and social group cohesion.

Another sign to look for are tree rubs. A bison will rub their horns on a tree to get the scent of the tree on themselves or to fight off insects.

Bison have a great sense of smell and aids in detecting predators. Bison also have keen hearing. They are able to detect moving objects from 2 km away and see large objects from 1 km away. Bison vocalize through grunts and snorts (Newell and Sorin, 2003).

Bison are great swimmers and are frequently seen crossing rivers during their travels.

Bison track on the prairie

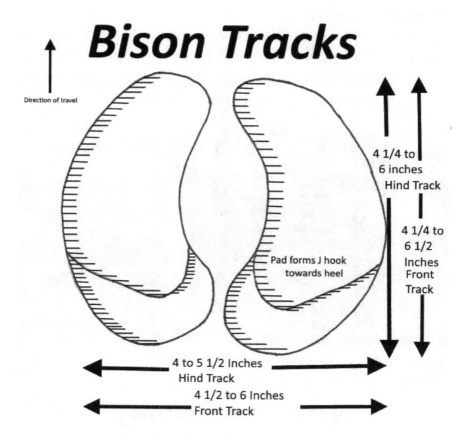

Bison Tracks

Direction of travel

4 1/4 to 6 inches Hind Track

4 1/4 to 6 1/2 Inches Front Track

Pad forms J hook towards heel

4 to 5 1/2 Inches Hind Track

4 1/2 to 6 Inches Front Track

The bison front track measures 4 ½ to 6 ½ inches in length and 4 ½ to 6 inches wide. The tracks are round. The interior hoof is concave for the entire length of the track. The front track is larger than the hind track which measures 4 ¼ to 6 inches in length and 4 to 5 ½ inches in width. These tracks are easily confused with domestic cows. The bison walk stride measures 22 to 38 inches in length and 10 to 22 inches in width. Their trot stride measures 40 to 44 inches in length and 10 to 15 inches in width (Elbroch, 2003)

Personal Tracking Record:
Front Track ☐   Hind Track ☐   Scat ☐

Other Sign Found: _____
Date Found: _____
Habitat Found: _____
Place Found: _____
Parent's Initials: _____

Personal Tracking Record:
Front Track ☐   Hind Track ☐   Scat ☐

Other Sign Found: _____
Date Found: _____
Habitat Found: _____
Place Found: _____
Parent's Initials: _____

Personal Tracking Record:
Front Track ☐   Hind Track ☐   Scat ☐

Other Sign Found: _____
Date Found: _____
Habitat Found: _____
Place Found: _____
Parent's Initials: _____

 Moose

Alces americanus

The moose is the largest living species in the deer family. The adult moose stands 4.6 feet to 6.9 feet at the shoulder. Bulls can weigh from 838 to 1,543 pounds. Cows can weigh between 441 and 1,080 pounds. They have thick brown fur that can be black to light in color. The individual hairs are hollow. This provides excellent insulation and aids in swimming. They have very long legs and a dewlap of skin that hangs from the throat. The moose is the second largest land animal in North America. They live between 15 and 22 years.

Moose Territory
IUCN Red List (2019)

Moose inhabit pine, spruce, and mixed **deciduous forests** (with trees that lose their leaves), of North America in **temperate climates** with moderate temperatures, no extremes of hot or cold, to subarctic climates. They can be found in Canada and Northern United States as far south as the Rocky Mountains of Colorado. They prefer forested areas with snow cover in the winter and available water. They require colder temperatures due to their difficulty with regulating their temperatures. They lack sweat glands and the fermentation to break down their food in their digestive systems produces heat.

Moose diet consists of both terrestrial and aquatic vegetation and fruit. They eat **aquatic plants** (plants that grow under water in lakes or rivers) for their salt. During winter they are drawn toward roadways to lick salt that is used to melt snow and ice. Moose lack upper front teeth but have eight sharp incisors on the lower jaw. They also have a tough tongue, lips, and gums that aid in eating woody vegetation. The moose's upper lip is very sensitive to help distinguish between fresh shoots and harder twigs. This lip is **prehensile,** (capable of grasping), for grabbing their food. They prefer new growths from deciduous trees with a high sugar content. They will sometimes stand on their hind legs to reach branches. They are the only deer that is capable of feeding under water. They are capable of closing their nostrils. The moose nose has fatty pads that close when exposed to water pressure. Moose are excellent swimmers. They wade into the water to eat, to cool down in summer, and to get rid of flies. They cannot digest hay, which explains they have never been domesticated.

Moose are solitary animals; they do not form herds. Although they generally are slow moving, they can move quickly when angered or startled. During the autumn the bulls can have impressive fights over a cow. The cow will select a bull based on the antler size. The size of antlers is based on the moose age and diet. Symmetry of antlers reflects good health. Their antlers are **palmate**, shaped like an open hand with the fingers extended that can measure up to 6 feet in width from tip to tip. The diameter of antlers, not the number of points, indicates age. After mating season, the bulls will drop their antlers to conserve energy for winter. New antlers grow in spring. Antlers take 3 to 5 months to fully develop making them one of the fastest growing animal organs.

Mating occurs in the fall. During the mating season both the cow and bull will call to each other. Cows can also give off a powerful scent to attract males. Bulls make grunting sounds and females will wail. The **gestation**, pregnancy, is 8 months. In May or June the females will bear one to two calves if food is plentiful. Newborn calves have reddish fur. They will stay with the mother until just before the next young are born. Moose calves are able to begin to browse and follow their mother at 3 weeks. They are weaned at 5 months. They are full grown at two years. Moose are solitary other than cow and calf. Cows are very protective of their calves and will charge people and use their hooves to strike.

Moose are diurnal, active during the daytime. Moose are able to run up to 35 miles per hour on land and swim up to 6 miles an hour. They have poor eyesight but have but makes up for this with an excellent sense of smell and hearing. They are able to locate food under the snow with this heightened sense of smell.

Moose scat measures ½ to 7/8 inches in diameter and 7/8 inch to 1 ¾ inches in length. They can also produce patties if they have been feeding on wetland vegetation.

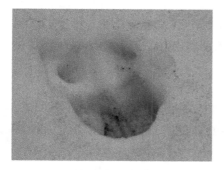

The moose front track measures 4 3/8 to 7 inches in length and 3 ¾ to 6 inches wide. They have two toes and 2 dew claws that are raised on the back of the leg.

Hooves are more heart shaped than elk tracks and point in the direction of travel. The interior of the hoof walls is concave for the front half of the track. Their front track is larger than their hind track. The hind track measures 4 1/8 to 6 ½ inches in length and 3 ½ to 4 5/8 inches in width.

The moose walking stride measures 28 to 44 inches in length and 8 ½ to 20 inches in width. The trot stride measures about 55 inches in length. The gallop stride measures 4 to 15 inches in length (Elbroch, 2003).

↑Moose Track

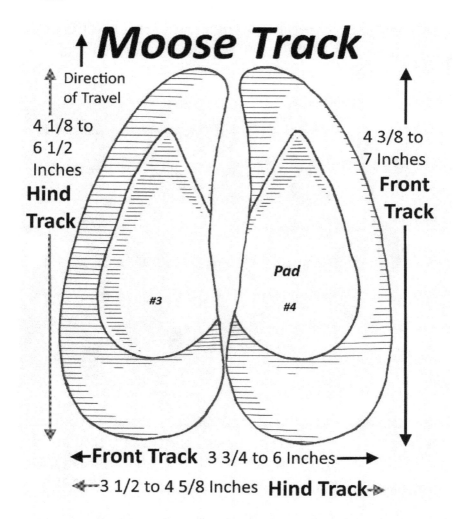

Direction of Travel

4 1/8 to 6 1/2 Inches
Hind Track

4 3/8 to 7 Inches
Front Track

Pad

#3

#4

◄Front Track 3 3/4 to 6 Inches **➔**

◄--3 1/2 to 4 5/8 Inches **Hind Track-»**

Do not include dew claws in the length measurement. Many times they do not show up in the track. The dew claws are toes #2 and #5. Toe #3 is a little smaller than toe #4. This indicates that this is the right hoof.

Personal Tracking Record:

Front Track ☐   Hind Track ☐   Scat ☐

Other Sign Found: _____

Date Found: _____

Habitat Found: _____

Place Found: _____

Parent's Initials: _____

Personal Tracking Record:

Front Track ☐   Hind Track ☐   Scat ☐

Other Sign Found: _____

Date Found: _____

Habitat Found: _____

Place Found: _____

Parent's Initials: _____

Personal Tracking Record:

Front Track ☐   Hind Track ☐   Scat ☐

Other Sign Found: _____

Date Found: _____

Habitat Found: _____

Place Found: _____

Parent's Initials: _____

 Caribou

Rangifer tarandus

Caribou, also commonly called reindeer, are a species of deer. Caribou are **ruminants,** meaning they chew their cud like cows do and they have four chambered stomaches using fermentation to aid in breaking down their food and use their special diet, which also helps them survive in winter. They mainly eat lichens in winter, an organism made up of cyanobacteria and fungus, which is not a plant but is usually found growing on rocks and trees.

Caribou Territory
IUCN Red List (2019)

They are one of only two animals in which the enzyme lichinase has been found. Lichenase breaks down lichens into glucose allowing the caribou to use them for energy. They will also eat leaves of willows and birches as well as sedges and grasses. When they are nutritionally stressed and their normal diet is not available, there is some evidence that they will eat small rodents such as lemmings, as well as fish, eggs, and mushroooms.

Caribou have many very specialized features. They can see wave-lengths of light as short as 320 nm (ultraviolet range), below the human threshold. The eyes of the artic caribou change color through the season from gold to deep blue to help them better detect predators.

Another adaptation is that caribou hooves adapt to the season. In summer when the tundra is soft and wet, their footpads become spongy and provide extra traction. In the winter their footpads shrink and tighten, exposing the rim of the hoof which aids in cutting into the ice and crusted snow and aids in traction. This also helps them dig down through the snow to their favorite food-a lichen known as reindeer moss.

Caribou migrate to exploit seasonal differences in the food availabe for them to browse or graze. Tundra vegetation has only a short summer growing season, but is highly nutritious. During winter caribou migrate to areas where they can dig through snow for lichens. They will migrate up to 3,000 miles, the furthest distance of any terrestrial animal. They also migrate to their calving grounds. This migration route is taught to the yearling calves.

The caribou have splayed hooves and strong legs that help them to walk on and dig in snow, swim, and migrate long distances. They also have long interdigital hairs between hooves, and glands that make a substance that prevents snow from clogging between their toes. They have a well-insulated coat made of hollow hairs. The air pockets in these hairs also enables them to swim high in the water. Their coat has two layers of hair; one is a dense wooly undercoat, while the other is a long-haired overcoat with hollow hairs. Additionally, caribou have specialized noses with nasal turbinate bones that dramatically increases the surface area within the nostril, which warms the cold air they breath before it enters their lungs. Their body will condense water from the air they breathe out before they exhale, and this water is used to moisten the dry incoming air.

The caribou is the only species of **cervid**, a member of the deer family, in which both sexes and their calves carry antlers. Their antlers have two separate groups of points, lower and upper. The antlers of a large male can be up to 39 inches in width and 53 inches in beam length. The color of caribou fur will also vary considerably depending on the season and what subspecies they are.

Caribou are able to run between 37 and 50 miles per hour. When preparing to mate, the males will battle for access to the females. They will lock antlers and push each other away. The dominant male will collect between 15 and 20 females.

Caribou scat is in pellets, which measure 3/8 to 5/8 inches in diameter and 3/8 to 7/8 inches in length.

It is very important to use a measuring tape to measure tracks. This will help with identification.

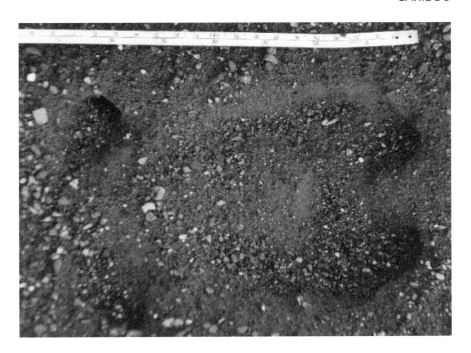

The caribou front track measures 3 ¼ inches to 5 inches in length and 4-6 inches in width. They are slightly asymmetrical. Their hooves are very rounded and tracks are round. The interior hoof walls are quite concave for the entire length of the track. The negative space in the center of the track is large. The caribou hind track measures 3 to 4 ½ inches in length and 3 5/8 to 4 ¾ inches in width. Both front and hind tracks usually show dew claws that become perpendicular to the direction of travel with the increased speed. When walking their stride will measure 23 to 33 inches. With a straddle trot, their stride measures 49 to 57 inches (Elbroch, 2003).

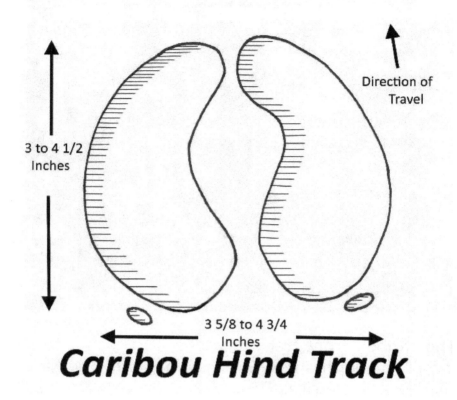

3 to 4 1/2 Inches

Direction of Travel

3 5/8 to 4 3/4 Inches

Caribou Hind Track

Do not include measuring the dew claws as part of the track length. Many times they do not show up in the track and the average track length does not include these dew claws.

Personal Tracking Record:

Front Track ☐   Hind Track ☐   Scat ☐

Other Sign Found: _____

Date Found: _____

Habitat Found: _____

Place Found: _____

Parent's Initials: _____

Personal Tracking Record:

Front Track ☐   Hind Track ☐   Scat ☐

Other Sign Found: _____

Date Found: _____

Habitat Found: _____

Place Found: _____

Parent's Initials: _____

Personal Tracking Record:

Front Track ☐   Hind Track ☐   Scat ☐

Other Sign Found: _____

Date Found: _____

Habitat Found: _____

Place Found: _____

Parent's Initials: _____

Pronghorn

Antilocapra americana

The pronghorn is one of the fastest animals on Earth. Pronghorn are technically not an antelope, but North Americans often call them pronghorn antelope. They can run up to 60 miles per hour and can maintain a speed of 45 miles per hour for more than 4 miles. Pronghorn have pointed cloven hooves that are cushioned to take the shock of a stride that may be 29 feet long at a full run. Generally pronghorn don't prefer to jump a fence, instead they will climb through a fence. This is because their legs are thin and more fragile.

Pronghorn have distinct white fur on their rump, on their sides, breasts, bellies and across their throats.

Adults , both males and females, measure 4 feet 3 inches to 4 feet 11 inches from their nose to tails and 32 to 41 inches high at the shoulder. Males weigh between 88 and 143 pounds. Females weigh between 75 and 106 pounds.

Pronghorn Antelope Territory
IUCN Red List (2019)

Pronghorn mainly live in valleys or plains, not in forests much. Their bodies are tan and white which is related to the use of the open prairie and brush lands. Males have black face markings beneath their chins. These markings are used in courtship and dominance displays. In Wyoming during summer and autumn, pronghorns have a range of 2.6 square kilometers to

5.2 square kilometers. Their range expands during winter to between 6.5 and 22.5 square kilometers. Whether or not a herd is territorial depends on rain. In areas with more than 16 inches of annual rain, producing better food, the pronghorn are territorial and mark their territory with scent markings, calling and challenging intruders. The males that defend their territories containing more protein-rich food get the most mates. Some females will return to the same territory to mate year after year. Pronghorn may travel in bachelor herds, in which only the dominant males breed.

Pronghorn are found in the western parts of the United States, Canada and parts of Mexico. They are diurnal, active during the daytime and through twilight. The pronghorn is unique among ruminants because of the permanent unbranched horn cores, in combination with a branched horn sheath that is shed anually. Both the males and females have black horns. The bucks have larger forward pointing prongs below the backward-pointing hooks. A doe has one horn that is smaller. The pronghorn has large protruding eyes that allows for 360 degrees of vision.

The pronghorn's teeth grow continuously. They feed primarily on forbes (non-grass herbs), shrubs and grasses. The males have nine skin glands. The two beneath the ears help mark their territory. Their rump glands produce alarm odors. Pronghorn are also able to show alarm by fluffing their white rump hair.

**Oops, caught this pronghorn in a private moment.
She was creating scat.**

Here is a proper picture of antelope scat, 3/16 to ½ inch in diameter and 3/8 to ¾ inch in length.

Pronghorn calves are easily camouflaged. They are frequently born as twins. These babies are only hours old.

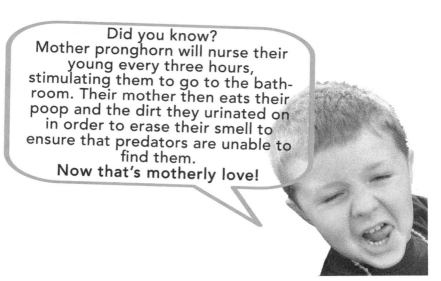

Did you know?
Mother pronghorn will nurse their young every three hours, stimulating them to go to the bathroom. Their mother then eats their poop and the dirt they urinated on in order to erase their smell to ensure that predators are unable to find them.
Now that's motherly love!

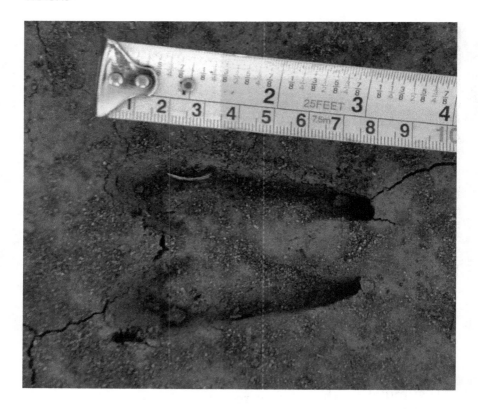

The pronghorn front track measures 2 1/8 to 3 ½ inches long and 1 ½ to 2 ¼ inches wide. Pronghorn lack dew claws. The hooves are heart shaped. The interior of the hooves are concave to the front of the track. The outside line of the track will also be slightly concave or straight in the center. Their toes will spread due to their speed or what they are walking in.

The hind track measures 2 ¼ to 3 ¼ inches long and 1 ½ inches to 2 1/8 inches wide (Elbroch, 2003).

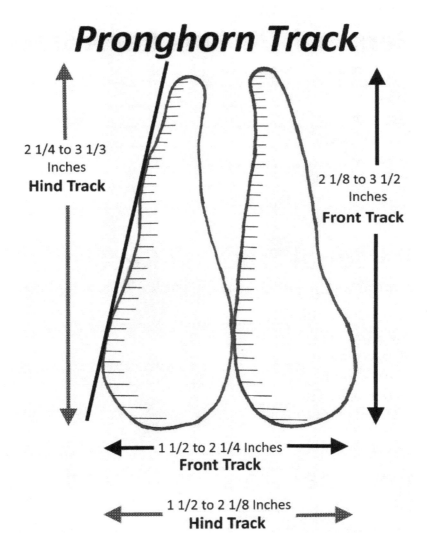

Pronghorn Track

2 1/4 to 3 1/3 Inches
Hind Track

2 1/8 to 3 1/2 Inches
Front Track

1 1/2 to 2 1/4 Inches
Front Track

1 1/2 to 2 1/8 Inches
Hind Track

The pronghorn's walking stride measures 17 to 26 inches in length and 4 3/8 to 10 inches wide. The pronghorn's overstep walking stride measures 19 to 29 inches in length. The pronghorn's bound or gallop stride measures 29 to 61 inches in length (Elbroch, 2003)

Personal Tracking Record:
Front Track ☐   Hind Track ☐   Scat ☐

Other Sign Found: _____
Date Found: _____
Habitat Found: _____
Place Found: _____
Parent's Initials: _____

Personal Tracking Record:
Front Track ☐   Hind Track ☐   Scat ☐

Other Sign Found: _____
Date Found: _____
Habitat Found: _____
Place Found: _____
Parent's Initials: _____

Personal Tracking Record:
Front Track ☐   Hind Track ☐   Scat ☐

Other Sign Found: _____
Date Found: _____
Habitat Found: _____
Place Found: _____
Parent's Initials: _____

 Mule Deer

Odocoileus hemionus

Adult mule deer in velvet, shedding his winter coat

Mule deer are 3.9 feet to 6.0 feet from nose to tail. Adult bucks weigh up to 460 pounds. Does weigh from 95 to 198 pounds. Mule deer are dark brown gray, light ash gray to brown and reddish in color. They have a black tip to their tail.

One of the most significant differences between mule deer and white-tailed deer is that the size of the mule deer's ears are larger. These large ears provide excellent hearing to assist in alerting for predators.

They also have excellent vision, where they can track another animal at 600 meters. Additionally, a mule deer has a black tip to its tail while the white-tailed deer has a brown tail with the underside being white along with its rump, so when it is startled it will raise it's tail as a warning to others. A last difference between mule deer and white-tailed deer is the configuration of their antlers. The mule deer's antlers are **bifurcated,** meaning they fork as they grow. They have scent glands that will mark who they are individually, mark for alarm, and leave a scent trail.

Even though they are capable of running, mule deer will **pronk**, a jump with all four feet coming down together. Mule deer will eat almost any vegetation including grass, fruits, and flowers, especially my flowers. They are considered **intermediate feeders** (feeds on grass and bushes) rather than solely being a **browser** (eats bushes) or a **grazer** (feeds on grasses). They are **ruminants**; before digestion, their stomachs ferment plant material in order to receive the nutrition from it.

Mule deer inhabit a wide variety of habitat including woodland chaparral of California, Mojave Sonoran desert, Interior semidesert shrub woodland, the Great Plains, the Colorado Plateau shrubland and forest, the Great Basin, the Sagebrush steepe, the Northern mountain and the Canadian boreal forrest (Wallmo, 1981)

Mule Deer IUCN Red List (2019)

The rut or "mating season" begins in the fall, primarily from late November to mid-December, whene the males will compete for females by fighting with their antlers. A buck will tend to a doe who is in **estrus** until they mate or he looses to another larger buck. Because the larger buck tends to have larger antlers, they are more successful with sparing, therefore they are more successful with mating. Does may mate with more than one buck. The buck's antlers fall off in the winter and almost immediately begin growing back.

Adult Mule Deer Doe

Like the white-tailed deer, mule deer typically give birth to only one young during their first year after maturity, then birthing twins every pregnancy after. They wean the fawns aroun 16 weeks of age.

Did you know?
Mother deer will nurse their young every couple of hours, stimulating them to go to the bathroom.
Their mother then eats their poop and the dirt they urinated on in order to erase their smell to ensure that predators are unable to find them.

Mule deer with establish a winter and summer home range that they continue to return to year after year. They migrate to summer home ranges higher in the elevation and winter home ranges, lower in elevation. The winter home ranges have more easily accessible food supply from less snow depth and with warmer temperatures. Herds consist of does that are related through maternal descent. These family clans will guard resources including food availability from other herds.

Mule deer have multiple techniques for avoiding predators. Their excellent hearing and vision detect predators from far off. They may choose to move into the bush to hide once they detect a predator. They may leave the area while the predator is still far off and move several miles. They may bound uphill to exhaust their predator. They may bound a short way, then trot off so they may gather more information. During this initial alarm bounding off, the deer can release from their toe scent glands an alarm scent that can actually inhibit feeding. This causes other mule deer to bound off as well. Lastly, when the predator is closing in, the mule deer will employ evasive maneuvers where they change their direction suddenly or get objects between itself and the predator.

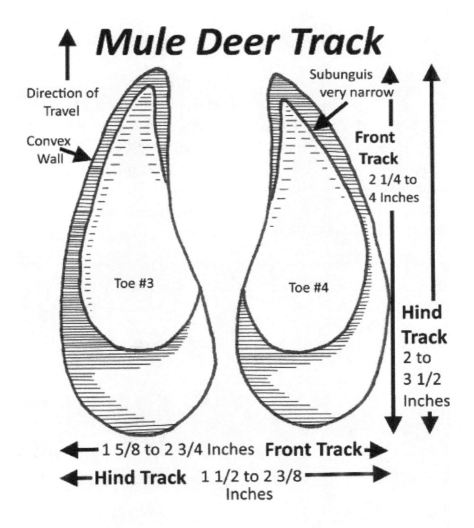

Mule Deer Track

Direction of Travel

Convex Wall

Subunguis very narrow

Front Track 2 1/4 to 4 Inches

Toe #3

Toe #4

Hind Track 2 to 3 1/2 Inches

1 5/8 to 2 3/4 Inches **Front Track**

Hind Track 1 1/2 to 2 3/8 Inches

Mule Deer front track measures 2 ¼ to 4 inches in length and 1 5/8 to 2 ¾ inches in width. At times in deep snow dew claws can be seen. The interior of the hoof walls are concave for the front half of the track.

121

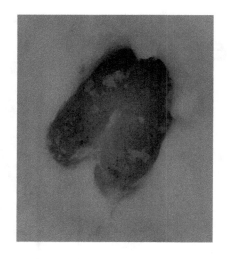

The hind track measures 2 to 3 ½ inches in length and 1 ½ to 2 3/8 inches in width. They are also heart shaped like the front track and point in the direction of travel (Elbroch, 2003). Do not include measuring the dew claws as part of the track length. Many times they don't show in the tracks.

Scat pellets measure 3/16 to 5/8 inches in diameter and ½ to 1 ¾ inches in length.

Personal Tracking Record:

Front Track ☐   Hind Track ☐   Scat ☐

Other Sign Found: _____

Date Found: _____

Habitat Found: _____

Place Found: _____

Parent's Initials: _____

Personal Tracking Record:

Front Track ☐   Hind Track ☐   Scat ☐

Other Sign Found: _____

Date Found: _____

Habitat Found: _____

Place Found: _____

Parent's Initials: _____

Personal Tracking Record:

Front Track ☐   Hind Track ☐   Scat ☐

Other Sign Found: _____

Date Found: _____

Habitat Found: _____

Place Found: _____

Parent's Initials: _____

 White-Tailed Deer

Odocoileus virginianus

White-tailed bucks after they have shed their antlers.

White-tailed deer are a medium-sized deer that range from Canada, through the United States and down to South America. They are able to adapt to a wide variety of habitats. The white-tailed deer's coat is a reddish brown in the spring and summer and turns gray-brown throughout the fall and winter. They have white on their throat, around their eyes and nose, on it's stomach and the underside of their tail. The buck's antlers branch from one main beam. The bucks lose their antlers in the winter after all of the females have mated. White-tailed deer are smaller than mule deer, the bucks weigh between 150 and 300 pounds. While does of both species weigh between 90 and 200 pounds.

White-tailed deer eat large amounts of food including legumes. They forage on other plants including shoots, leaves, cacti, grasses, acorns, fruit, and corn. Their specialized stomaches allow them to eat mushrooms and poison ivy. They have also been seen feeding opportunistically on nesting songbirds and mice. Like the mule deer, they are also ruminants with four-chambered stomachs, and the ability to ferment and digest differt types of food.

White-Tailed Deer
IUCN Red List (2019)

White-tailed deer are able to thrive in a wide variety of habitats. They are found in the woods of Northern Maine to the hammock swamps of Florida, farmlands, brush areas and even the cactus and thornbrush deserts in Texas..

White-tailed deer respond to a predator by breathing heavily, also known as blowing, stomping their hooves and fleeing. This blowing alerts other deer in the area. As they run they flash their white tails to warn other deer. They are able to jump 8.9 feet high and up to 33 feet in length. They can run up to 30 miles per hour. They do not typically **pronk**, jumping with all four feet at a time, like the mule deer. They are adept swimmers and will swim to evade predators or swim to an island. They do not migrate during the winter. They will bed down during the day but will not use the same bed where they have been previously.

Bucks do not guard a harem but will fight other bucks individually for an individual doe. Bucks mate with multiple does, **polygamous**. The **rut**, (mating period) for bucks begins in October and lasts until December. Bucks compete for breeding with does. They spar to determine a dominance heirarchy. The bucks attempt to mate with as many females as possible. This practice can even make them lose physical conditioning since they rarely eat or rest during the rut. Does begin mating triggered mainly by the declining photoperiod, the shorter amount of daylight in the fall.

In the first year, a doe will have one fawn. After the second year, they usually have twins. The fawns will stand within an hour of birth and are immediately walking. They will begin to eat vegetation within only a few days. They are weaned between 8 and 10 weeks old. White-tailed does are protective of their fawns. They will leave their fawns in a hiding place for a few hours at a time while they are foraging. The fawns will lay flat, barely moving until their mother's return. The young will hold both their urine and feces until their mother returns. When she nurses them, they void and then the mother eats their feces and urine to hide her fawn's smell from predators. They are not strong or fast enough to outrun predators and their safest defence is hiding. When they are about four weeks old they are strong enough to follow their mother foraging. Males leave their mother after the first year, females leave their mother after two years.

White-Tailed Doe

Not even going to move to get rid of the fly on its forehead.
Photo courtesy of Jerry Abbie

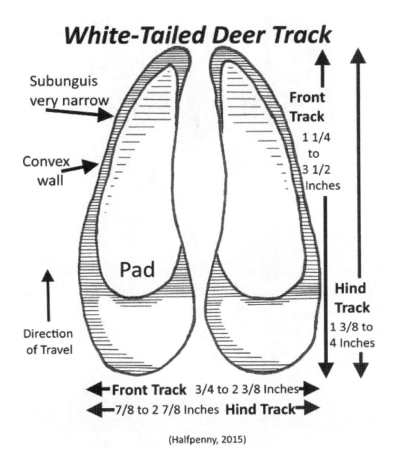

White-Tailed Deer Track

Subunguis very narrow

Convex wall

Pad

Front Track 1 1/4 to 3 1/2 Inches

Hind Track 1 3/8 to 4 Inches

Direction of Travel

← Front Track 3/4 to 2 3/8 Inches →

← 7/8 to 2 7/8 Inches Hind Track →

(Halfpenny, 2015)

White-tailed deer front track measures 1 3/8 to 4 inches in length and 7/8 to 2 7/8 inches wide. One hoof is slightly smaller than the other. Hooves are heart shaped. The interior walls of the hoof are concave for the front half of the track.

The hind track measures 1 ¼ to 3 ½ inches in length and ¾ to 2 3/8 wide (Elbroch, 2003).

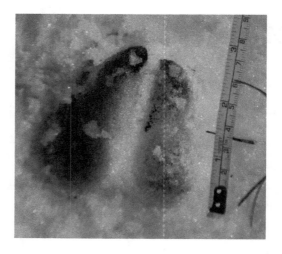

The white-tailed deer walking stride measures 13 to 26 inches in length and 4 to 10 inches wide. The trotting stride measures 29 to 56 inches in length and 2 to 4 inches wide. The white tailed deer bound or gallop stride measures 6 to 20 feet in length (Elbroch, 2003).

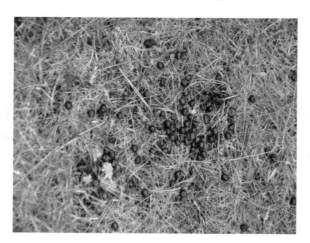

White-tailed deer pellets measure 3/16 to 5/8 inches in diameter and ½ to 1 ¾ inches in length.

Personal Tracking Record:
Front Track ☐   Hind Track ☐   Scat ☐

Other Sign Found: _____
Date Found: _____
Habitat Found: _____
Place Found: _____
Parent's Initials: _____

Personal Tracking Record:
Front Track ☐   Hind Track ☐   Scat ☐

Other Sign Found: _____
Date Found: _____
Habitat Found: _____
Place Found: _____
Parent's Initials: _____

Personal Tracking Record:
Front Track ☐   Hind Track ☐   Scat ☐

Other Sign Found: _____
Date Found: _____
Habitat Found: _____
Place Found: _____
Parent's Initials: _____

Elk

Cervus canadensis

Bull elk in early spring, still in velvet

Elk live in forest and edge-of-forest habitat. They are considered very adaptable and have been introduced into other countries. They will **migrate** (travel to different habitats depending on the season) to higher elevations in the spring, following the retreating snow line and then migrate to lower elevations in the winter. The bull elk, male, can weigh between 705 and 730 pounds and will be a little lighter in color, while a cow elk can weigh between 496 to 531 pounds. Cows measure 6.9 feet from nose to tail while a bull can meaure 8 feet from nose to tail. Elk are the second largest animal of the deer family with only the moose being larger. They are brown to reddish brown with a buff colored rump. The Rocky Mountain Elk have darker brown necks and heads during the winter, almost giving them appearance of a mane.

Elk Territory
IUCN Red List (2019)

As elk calves are born with spots, using camoflage as a primary defense from predators. When first born, the elk calves do not have the strength or speed to outrun predators. Elk calves are protected by being left alone for hours, for the first few weeks following birth, while their mother **forages** in the distance, within hearing range but not within sight. Their spots camoflage as the calves lay in the brush waiting for their mothers. Scientists believe that by foraging away from the calf, the mother is ensuring she doesn't bring direct attention from predators to where their calves are. Newborn calves are easy prey for bears, cougars and wolves. Elk mothers return only at intervals to nurse their young, until their young are strong enough to follow them during foraging. A calf only comes out when called by its mother. They will also duck down and freeze upon their monther's cue to hide from predators, not moving a muscle.

During the fall the elk will grow a thicker coat of hair to help them survive the winter. During the spring they will rub on trees to help them shed this coat of hair. Bull elk grow antlers in the spring and shed them in the winter. These are true antlers and are made of bone. When antlers initially grown in, they are covered in a velvet. Once they are grown in, the elk will rub on tree to assist in shedding this velvet leaving the hardened bone. Elk may have as many as eight tines on each antler. These antlers can measure up to 3.9 feet long. However, the size and number of tines on an antler does not indicate the age of the bull. Elk will live between 10 to 13 years.

Elk are ruminants, meaning they have four-chambered stomaches and chew their cud. They feed on grasses, plants, leaves, and bark. During the summer they will eat almost constantly in order to help them bulk up to survive the winter when food is scarcer. When feeding in the open, the majority of the elk herd will be feeding with their heads down, however at least one or two will be on sentry duty with their heads up and on alert, scanning all around for danger.

A yearling elk with its maternal herd

The adult elk usually stay with single-sex groups for most of the year. The cow herd will also include the calves and one bull. During mating, the **rut**, bulls will compete for the cows and will try to defend the females already in their harem. Dominant bulls will keep a larger harem of cows and restrict other bull's access to them. They will antler wrestle, pee on them-selves, or urinate on the ground and roll their bodies in it, and bugle to attract females. These harems usually include 1 bull and 6 cows with their yearly calves. The bulls will defend these harems by fighting intruders. These boutes can be intense, result in exhaustion and injury or death. Other males will spend the rut on the outside edges of the larger harems.

The cows give birth to one calf at a time. A cow and her calf will live alone for several weeks. They rejoin the herd at 16 days and the mother will wean her calf within 2 months.

Cow elk with new calf only hours old
Elk calves are born with spots

While you are outdoors working on identifying the animal tracks you can often hear elk communicating. Bull elk will bugle to attract cows for mating. This bugling also warns other bulls that he is ready to fight for his girls. This bugling sounds like a bellow that escalates to a squealing whistle and ends with a grunt. Elk will bark as a danger warning. The newborn calf will use a high-pitched squeal. Her mother is able to recognize her voice. Additionally, elk will mew, chirp and have miscellaneous squeals as general conversation in the herd. Elk communicate with body postures as well. When they are alarmed and listening for danger they will raise their head up high moving their ears to listen. If one of his cows in his harem begins to wander the bull elk will stretch his neck out low, tip up his nose and tilt his head and antlers back, then circle her. Elk will curl their upper lip back, grind their teeth and hiss softly as a threat to each other.

An elk showing agitation will lay their ears back, flare their nostrils, hold their heads up high and punch with their front hooves.

Elk pellets measure 7/16 to 11/16 inches in diameter and ½ to 1 inch in length.

Did you know that Elk can poop up to 20 times a day!!

Did you know? Bull elk will pee on themselves in order to attract females.
Gross!!

Here is an elk rub where the bull rubbed on a tree branch to shed his velvet off his antlers.

Elk will avoid dense unbroken forests and choose open woodlands. Elk habitats include coniferous swamps, coniferous-hardwood forests, clear cuts and aspen-hardwood forests. They are found from sea level to 9,000 feet. Elk will live in the summer in herds up to 400 animals. These herds are matriarchal with a single cow as the lead. They browse in the early morning and later evening. They are not active during the day and can be seen down and resting and chewing their cud.

Elk Track

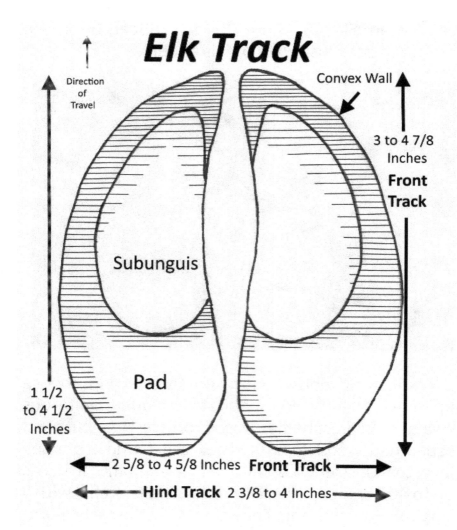

Direction of Travel

Convex Wall

3 to 4 7/8 Inches

Front Track

Subunguis

Pad

1 1/2 to 4 1/2 Inches

◄— 2 5/8 to 4 5/8 Inches **Front Track** —►

◄——— **Hind Track** 2 3/8 to 4 Inches ——►

The front track measures 3 to 4 7/8 inches in length and 2 5/8 to 4 5/8 inches wide. Their tracks are rounded, sometimes pointed with wider tips. The front track is larger than the rear track. The two toes will spread depending on speed.

The hind track measures 2 ½ to 4 ½ inches in length and 2 3/8 to 4 inches wide (Elbroch, 2003).

Myth busters: You cannot accurately determine the sex of the elk by the size of the track. One hint you can look at is the depth of the toe of the track versus the heel. If the heel is deeper it is more likely to be a bull elk because of their heavier weight.

Personal Tracking Record:

Front Track ☐   Hind Track ☐   Scat ☐

Other Sign Found: _____
Date Found: _____
Habitat Found: _____
Place Found: _____
Parent's Initials: _____

Personal Tracking Record:

Front Track ☐   Hind Track ☐   Scat ☐

Other Sign Found: _____
Date Found: _____
Habitat Found: _____
Place Found: _____
Parent's Initials: _____

Personal Tracking Record:

Front Track ☐   Hind Track ☐   Scat ☐

Other Sign Found: _____
Date Found: _____
Habitat Found: _____
Place Found: _____
Parent's Initials: _____

 Wild Boar

Sus scrofa

Piglet

The wild boar is a massively built **suid** (pig family) with short thin legs. Its trunk is short and bulky while its hindquarters are smaller. Behind the shoulder blades is a hump with a short thick neck. The boar has a large head that comprises one third of the length of its body. Its powerful neck muscles work perfectly with a head that acts like a plow. This combination can allow them to dig four inches into frozen ground and upturn rocks up to 110 pounds. They have long wide ears and small eyes. The wild boar's color can be variable ranging from black to brownish-red to white. They can also range from being solid in color to speckled. They can range in size from 59 inches to 95 inches long. They can weigh between 145 pounds to 600 pounds. They can run up to 25 miles per hour and are able to jump up to 59 inches high. Males have a mane running down their backs. The male's canine teeth are also more prominent. They can live up to 9 years in the wild.

Sus scrofa Territory
U.S. Department of Agriculture National Invasive
Species Information Center (2019)

The Wild boar can be very dangerous. They are considered the 4th most intelligent animal in the world.

If they are wounded by a predator, they are known to circle the predator, and charge from behind. They can have razor sharp tusks.

The wild boar is an invasive species that was initially introduced to the Hawaiian Islands by the Polynesians when they traveled there almost 800 years ago. The wild boar has also been introduced to a number of states in the lower 48. They have cross-bred with the feral (wild) pigs. Wild pigs have been reported in 44 states. They inhabit diverse habitats from boreal forests (northern) to deserts. They require three conditions to survive in a habitat: heavily brushed areas for shelter from predators; water for drinking and bathing; and an absence of regular snowfall. They are known to be good swimmers capable of swimming long distances. They can be found in grassy savanna habitat, wooded forests, agricultural areas, shrublands and marshy swampland. Although they thrive in multiple climates, they tend to avoid extreme heat or cold.

Wild boars are invasive and survive well not only because they are well adapted to varying habitats but also because of their very adaptable diet. They are omnivores. They will eat rhizomes, roots, tubers and bulbs which they are able to dig up throughout the year. They also eat nuts, berries, seeds, leaves, bark, twigs, and shoots. Additionally, wild boars eat earthworms, insects, mollusks, fish, rodents, bird eggs, lizards, snakes, frogs, carrion and garbage. The majority of their food is dug from the ground, usually plant material and burrowing animals.

Wild boars live in matriarchal groups consisting of females and their young called **sounders** and can include from 6 to 20 individuals. These sounders include **sows**, females, that have not yet begun breeding, young mothers with their young and is led by an old matriarch. Adult males, **boars,** are usually solitary. Males leave their sounder between the age of 8 and 15 months. Female never leave their sounder. They breed from November to January. Prior to mating, the males develop a subcutaneous armor, under the skin. Once ready to reproduce the male will travel to search for a sounder of sows. Once they find the group, the males chase off the young and pursue the sows. While in the **rut**, the males will fiercely fight off rivals. During this period the males eat little and can lose up to 20% of their body weight. Boars will chase a sow when interested in mating and nudge them. If the sow is interested, she will urinate, how romantic.

Wild boars can reproduce at any time of the year. Mating is dependent on the climate and food availability. Sows can begin mating at 10 months old. Sows can produce multiple litters with 5 to 6 piglets a year. The sows construct a nest with twigs, grasses and leaves to birth her piglets. If the mother dies prematurely the piglets are adopted by other sows in the sounder. The piglets do not leave the nest for the first week of life. They are weaned between 8 and 12 weeks. They are fully grown at 5 years old. When the sounder is on the move, the adult sows will travel in front and in the rear, keeping the piglets in between. The piglets are usually left with one babysitter while the other sows are foraging.

Depending on the climate, wild boars can be active both at day and at night. In warmer climates they tend to be more active during the night, so they can remain cool in the shade or wallowing in mud or water to stay cool. This not only cools them but protects them from mosquitos and can remove parasites. When feeding during the daytime, the wild boar tends to stay in more covered areas protecting them from predators, they will wait until evening to move to the open areas to feed.

The wild boar's front track measures 2 1/8 inches to 2 5/8 inches in length and 2 ¼ to 3 inches in width. Their front tracks are larger than the hind tracks. The rear tracks measure 1 7/8 to 2 ½ inches in length and 2 to 2 ¾ inches in width. Their walking stride measures 13 to 17 inches with a stride width between 7 to 8 ½ inches. The loping stride measures 36 to 52 inches (Elbroch, 2003).

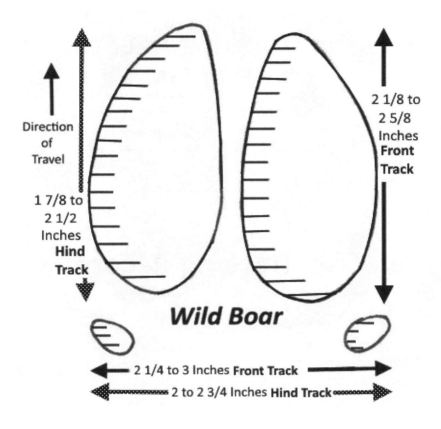

Direction of Travel

2 1/8 to 2 5/8 Inches **Front Track**

1 7/8 to 2 1/2 Inches **Hind Track**

Wild Boar

2 1/4 to 3 Inches **Front Track**

2 to 2 3/4 Inches **Hind Track**

Personal Tracking Record:

Front Track ☐   Hind Track ☐   Scat ☐

Other Sign Found: _____
Date Found: _____
Habitat Found: _____
Place Found: _____
Parent's Initials: _____

Personal Tracking Record:

Front Track ☐   Hind Track ☐   Scat ☐

Other Sign Found: _____
Date Found: _____
Habitat Found: _____
Place Found: _____
Parent's Initials: _____

Personal Tracking Record:

Front Track ☐   Hind Track ☐   Scat ☐

Other Sign Found: _____
Date Found: _____
Habitat Found: _____
Place Found: _____
Parent's Initials: _____

 # Snowshoe Hare

Lepus americanus

Snowshoe hares' primary habitat is northern forests. One of the shyest of hares, they rest by day in a hollow log or a woodchuck hole. They can run up to 30 miles per hour with bounds of 10 feet. They try to hide in brush rather than run in the open. They thump with their hind foot on the ground to send an alarm and warn other hares of danger. Even though they are good swimmers, they try to avoid water. They frequently will use a grouse wallow to take a dust bath.

Snowshoe Hare Territory
IUCN Red List (2019)

During the summer, they are dark brown with a small tail, dark above and white on the underside. In the winter, they go through what is called a seasonal molt that changes their coat and become white with mottled brown. This seasonal **molt,** when they shed one coat of hair and grown in another, is triggered by the seasonal lengthening and shortening amounts of daylight. They have black-tipped moderately long ears and large hind feet with the soles well furred especially in the winter. Even if the snow comes unusually late in fall or lasts an unusually long time in the spring, the hare will still have **molted,** In these situations, they can stand out instead of being **camouflaged** and blending in with their environment. In these situations, they could be mostly white in late fall regardless of lack of snow, and dark brown in the spring even if the ground is still snow covered. When the hare is less camouflaged it will become less active and seek more cover.

In the summer, they will feed on grasses, green vegetation, willow, and berries. In the winter they eat conifer buds, and the bark of aspen trees, alders and willow trees.

The primary difference between rabbits and a hares relate to how they avoid predators and how they reproduce. Snowshoe hares, with their longer legs, will try to outrun predators and can reach up to 30 miles per hour. Shorter-limbed rabbits will hide in dense cover or burrows to avoid predators. Hares have a longer gestation (time when the mothers are pregnant), and the young are better developed at birth compared with rabbits. Snowshoe hare babies, called kittens, are able to run within one hour of being born and are born with full fur and open eyes. They are usually born under brush. Burrowing rabbits have a shorter gestation and their babies are born naked with their eyes still closed. Snowshoe hares usually nurse for one, 5 minute period every twenty-four hours. They only nurse for the first three weeks of life. The mother will leave the young for most of the day in order to avoid bringing predators back to her kittens.

Both rabbits and hares have large eyes that are adapted to being **nocturnal**, out at night, and **crepuscular,** out during dawn and dusk. Most hares, other than snowshoe hares, prefer open habitats with some cover. Snowshoe hares may burrow in the snow. Snowshoe hares rely more heavily on scent for communication than they do sound. They have scent glands in the groin and under the chin.

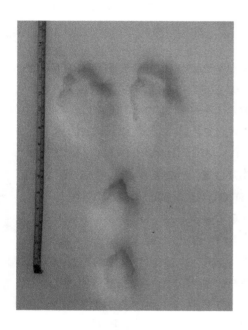

The snowshoe hare front track measures 1 7/8 to 3 inches long and 1 1/8 to 2 ¼ inches in width. They are very asymmetrical. There are 5 toes. Toe # 1 is much smaller but has a claw and occasionally shows in tracks. The tracks are pointy. The bottom of the foot is furred and may not show pads in the track. The front track is significantly smaller than the rear track. The hind track measures 3 ¼ to 6 inches in length and 1 5/8 to 5 inches wide. They have four toes and are also asymmetrical. The bottom of their hind feet is furred also and may not show toe pads in the snow. Their tracks are rounder than those of other rabbits.

The snowshoe bounding stride measures 8 to 72 inches and up to 10 feet. The trail width is 3 ¾ to 10 inches (Elbroch, 2003).

Front Track

1 7/8 to 3 Inches

1 1/8 to 2 1/4 Inches

Hind Track

Snowshoe

Hare

3 1/4 to 6 Inches

1 5/8 to 5 Inches

Snowshoe hare scat is perfectly round small pellets shown above. The scat generally measures 3/8 to 11/16 inches in diameter.

Personal Tracking Record:

Front Track ☐   Hind Track ☐   Scat ☐

Other Sign Found: _____
Date Found: _____
Habitat Found: _____
Place Found: _____
Parent's Initials: _____

Personal Tracking Record:

Front Track ☐   Hind Track ☐   Scat ☐

Other Sign Found: _____
Date Found: _____
Habitat Found: _____
Place Found: _____
Parent's Initials: _____

Personal Tracking Record:

Front Track ☐   Hind Track ☐   Scat ☐

Other Sign Found: _____
Date Found: _____
Habitat Found: _____
Place Found: _____
Parent's Initials: _____

 Mountain Cottontail Rabbit

Sylvilagus nuttalli

The mountain cottontail is a small. Its hind feet are long and covered in thick long hair. The cottontail's ears are rounded at the tips and somewhat short, with the inner surfaces covered with fur. It has pale brown fur on its back, a pale brown nape on the back of the neck, black-tipped ears, and a white gray tail with the white underside. The snowshoe hare and the mountain cottontail are distinguished by the brown nape on the back of the cottontail's neck.

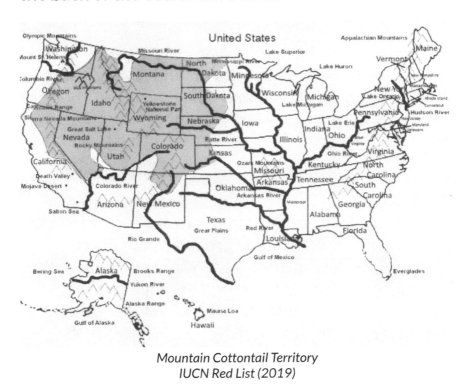

Mountain Cottontail Territory
IUCN Red List (2019)

The primary differences between a rabbit and a hare are how they avoid predators and how they reproduce. The longer-legged hare will try to outrun the predator, and some hares can reach up to 45 miles per hour. Shorter-legged rabbits will hide in dense cover or burrows to avoid predators. Hares have a longer gestation, (time when the mothers are pregnant), and their young are better developed at birth compared with rabbits. Snowshoe hare babies, called kittens, are able to run within one hour of being born and are born with full fur and open eyes. They are usually born under brush. Burrowing rabbits have a shorter gestation and their babies are born naked with their eyes still closed.

The mountain cottontail makes a nest that is a cup-shaped cavity (hole) lined with fur and dried grass. The female places fur, grass, and small sticks on the top. The breeding season varies during the period from February through July. The average litter size is four to six kits.

The lifespan of the cottontail averages two years. The cottontail is prey to almost every carnivore that is larger or faster but the greatest threat are birds of prey. The newborn kits are the most vulnerable. The mother is unable to defend her kits. Even though mated pairs of cottontails have multiple litters of kits, only a few will survive to adulthood. The kits that do survive are full grown adults at three months.

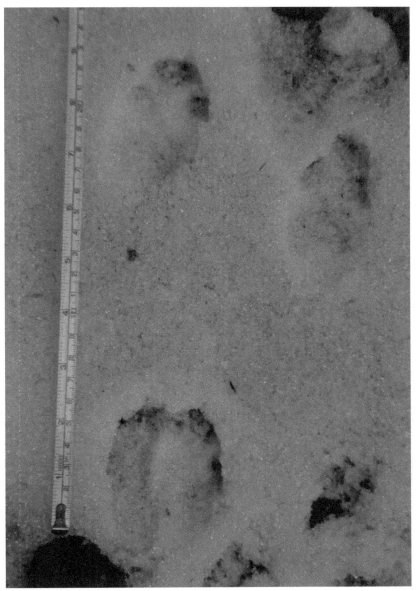

Mountain Cottontail tracks

The front track measures 1 to 1 7/8 inches in length and measures ¾ to 1 3/8 inches in width. The tracks

are pointy. The pads are furred and fur marks are often seen in the tracks. The nails may or may not show up. The front tracks are much smaller than the rear tracks.

The rear tracks measure 1 ¼ to 3 ¼ inches long and 7/8 to 1 13/16 inches wide.

The bounding stride measures between 5 and 32 inches. The trail width measures 2 ¼ to 5 inches.The group length measures 6 to 18 inches (Elbroch, 2003).

A group length is the distance from the heel of the furthest back foot to the tip of the furthest forward foot that includes both front feet and both hind feet. In this photo the group length is about 9 inches. The two tracks towards the bottom of the picture are the front feet. The hind feet have to go around the front feet and will be further apart. This shows that this rabbit was in a bound because the front feet in the track appear to be behind the hind tracks in the direction of travel. Rabbits and hares are known actually to have a half bound regularly because their front feet usually don't land directly together.

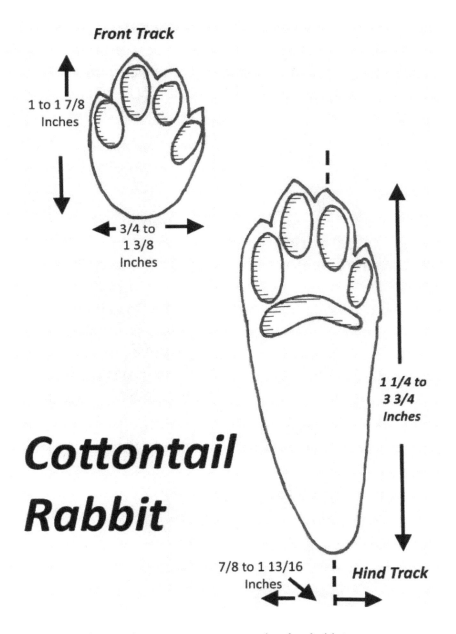

Front Track

1 to 1 7/8 Inches

3/4 to 1 3/8 Inches

Cottontail Rabbit

1 1/4 to 3 3/4 Inches

7/8 to 1 13/16 Inches

Hind Track

Cottontail tracks are assymetrical- 1 ½ toes on one side and 2 ½ toes on the other.

These rabbits are active in the early morning and late afternoon, **crepuscular**. They are not a typically social species of rabbit, more solitary. They can be found in groups if food is plentiful. More than 50% of their time is spent feeding. The mountain cottontail diet is mostly grasses including wheatgrasses, needle and thread, Indian grasses, cheatgrass brome, bluegrasses, and bottlebrush squirreltail. Depending on their habitat, their diet may include shrubs suchs as big sagebrush, rabbitbrush and saltbrushes. When food becomes more limited during winter months, the cottontail may eat more woody plants such as bark and twigs.

Did you know?
Rabbits will eat their own scat. This is to recolonize their intestines with bacteria to help them digest cellulose (plants).

Personal Tracking Record:

Front Track ☐   Hind Track ☐   Scat ☐

Other Sign Found: _____
Date Found: _____
Habitat Found: _____
Place Found: _____
Parent's Initials: _____

Personal Tracking Record:

Front Track ☐   Hind Track ☐   Scat ☐

Other Sign Found: _____
Date Found: _____
Habitat Found: _____
Place Found: _____
Parent's Initials: _____

Personal Tracking Record:

Front Track ☐   Hind Track ☐   Scat ☐

Other Sign Found: _____
Date Found: _____
Habitat Found: _____
Place Found: _____
Parent's Initials: _____

 American Pika

Ochotona princeps

The American pika is a rabbit with a grayish to cinnamon-brown oval shaped body with short dark ears that have a white edge, short legs, no visible tail and long **vibrissae,** whiskers. They have very sharp hearing, a wide field of vision and keen depth perception. They weigh between 121 to 176 grams around 6 ounces. The American pika's body length is between 6.4 and 8.5 inches. Their color varies by season. The

American pika molts twice a year and its winter coat is more grayish with longer hair. They have back paws with four toes that are **digitigrade**, walking on its toes. Their paws have dense fur except small naked black pads on their toes. They have a high metabolic rate that causes their average body temperature to be 104 degrees Fahrenheit. This metabolic rate causes them to have to manage their temperatures by behavior rather than their bodies being able to cool themselves down. They have a low lethal temperature and will die if their bodies hit 109.5 degrees Fahrenheit. Males are called bucks and females are called does. Males are slightly larger than females. The average life span is 3 to 4 years.

American Pika Territory
IUCN Red List (2019)

The American pika is a **diurnal,** meaning they are out during the daytime. The American pika's habitat is in boulder fields, rockslides and in mining tailings at or above the tree line. They can be found throughout the mountains of western North America. They have their den or nest beneath rocks that are 0.2 to 1 meter in diameter but they will sit on larger rocks. They do not dig burrows but will enlarge their home by digging. They are intolerant of high daily temperatures but they may be found near sea level in the norther part of their habitat. In the southern portion of their range, they are rarely seen below 8,200 feet in elevation.

Because the American pika does not hibernate, it will prepare for the winter by **haying.** They are herbivores and eat a large variety of plants including grasses, sedges, thistles and fireweed. In one day, pika will make up to 100 trips for haying. Pika will cache food in hay-piles to save for the winter. These hay-piles will be moved during the seasons to avoid rain and moisture. The pika is able to meet its need for water from the plants that they eats; however they do drink water if it is available and accessible.

Adult pikas of the opposite sex with territories next to each other will form a mated pair. They are monogamous. They are solitary until mating. They start breeding about one month before the snow melts. The **gestation**, pregnancy is 30 days.

The female has two litters a year averaging three young each. They are born blind, having only slight amount of hair but with full teeth. They are able to open their eyes around 9 days old. The mothers forage for most of the day but return to nurse their young every two hours. The babies are weaned and become independent when they are 4 weeks old. After three months they are fully grown. They may stay in their mother's home range, but they will occupy areas away from their relatives as much as possible.

Pikas are vocal and will call to warn of predators nearby. Males will sing during the breeding season. When you are standing close to a rockslide and you hear chirping coming from different directions this is a good sign that you are in pika territory.

The American pika's front track measures between 11/16 to 7/8 inches in length and 11/16 to 7/8 inches in width. They have five toes but toe # 1 is smaller and may not show in a track. The tracks are round, and the sole is furred. The hind track measures ¾ to 1 1/8 inches in length and ¾ to 1 inch wide. The hind track has four toes. The bound stride measures 2 ¼ to 15 inches in length. The group length measures 2 to 4 7/8 inches long (Elbroch, 2003).

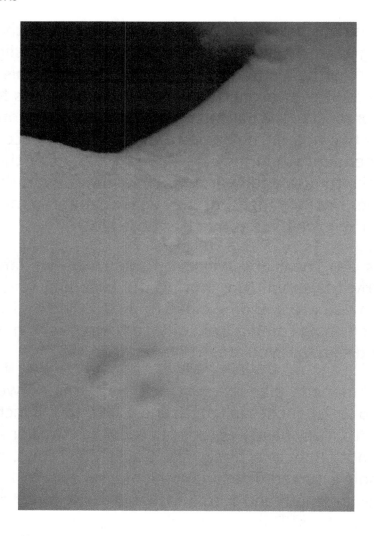

This pika track shows nice hops where it was in no hurry. This is obvious because the hind feet are shown in the track behind the front feet in the group. This track leads to the tunnels beneath large boulders.

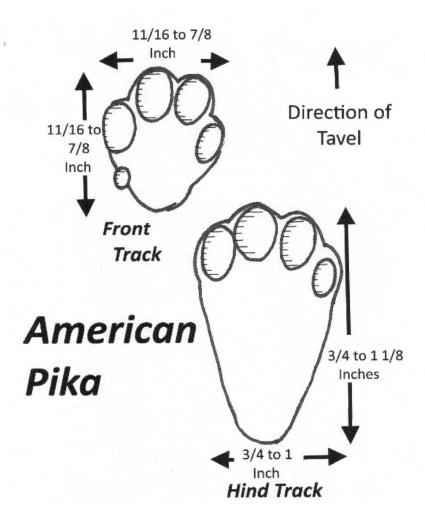

11/16 to 7/8 Inch

11/16 to 7/8 Inch

Direction of Tavel

Front Track

American Pika

3/4 to 1 1/8 Inches

3/4 to 1 Inch

Hind Track

Personal Tracking Record:
Front Track ☐   Hind Track ☐   Scat ☐

Other Sign Found: _____
Date Found: _____
Habitat Found: _____
Place Found: _____
Parent's Initials: _____

Personal Tracking Record:
Front Track ☐   Hind Track ☐   Scat ☐

Other Sign Found: _____
Date Found: _____
Habitat Found: _____
Place Found: _____
Parent's Initials: _____

Personal Tracking Record:
Front Track ☐   Hind Track ☐   Scat ☐

Other Sign Found: _____
Date Found: _____
Habitat Found: _____
Place Found: _____
Parent's Initials: _____

 Beaver

Castor canadensis

Juvenile North American beaver

The North American beaver can weigh between forty four and sixty six pounds and is usually active in the late afternoon and at night. Beavers are considered semi-aquatic and they have multiple fascinating features including.

- They are able to seal their nostrils and ears when they submerge.
- They can remain submerged for up to 15 minutes.
- They have a **nictitating membrane**, a see-through membrane, that covers their eyes allowing them to see underwater.

- They have a thick layer of fat under the skin that insulates from the cold water.
- They have webbed back feet, making them excellent swimmers. Their front paws are smaller and have long claws.
- They have a large flat tail that they use to signal danger by slapping the surface of the water.
- They have scent glands near their genitals that secretes an oily substance called castoreum, which they use to waterproof their fur.
- They can swim up to five miles an hour.

Beaver Territory
IUCN Red List (2019)

The beaver is considered a **keystone species**, a species that other animals rely on for their habitat. They build dams in small streams, creating ponds on which other wildlife rely to live. After they build the dam across the stream, they will build a lodge to live in. The surrounding water provides their homes protection. The lodges are oven shaped and typically have two rooms. The first room is for drying off and has two entrances. One entrance is more steep descent into the water while the other is more gradual and opens to the center of the room. The second room may measure up to eight feet wide and three feet high. The floor is covered with bark, grass and wood chips. There is usually a small air hole in the top of the lodge. These lodges are built with sticks, grass, moss woven together and plastered with mud.

Beavers can build three styles of lodge, island lodges, lodges on the banks of ponds and lodges built on the shores of lakes. A pond lodge is built a short distance from the bank of the pond with the front wall built from the bottom of the pond. The lake lodge is built on underwater shelving from the lake. The island lodge has a central chamber with the floor above the water level. They use their front paws for digging and placing their materials.

Some beavers will live in burrows dug in the riverbank. They construct their lodges out of sticks, twigs, logs, rocks and mud. The beaver can move up to four hundred pounds of wood a day!

Beavers eat twigs and bark. They store twigs in the mud outside the lodge by sharpening one end of the branch and shoving it in the mud on the pond bottom. This fridge keeps their food fresh for the winter. They eat the inner bark, the **cambium**, twigs, shoots and leaves. In the spring and summer, they eat leaves, roots, herbs, ferns, grasses and algae. They eat more shrubs and trees in the fall. Aspen is their preferred tree diet. Beavers are rare in that they are able to digest the cellulose in these wooded plants with the assistance of microorganisms in their intestines. Beavers will travel long distances from their pond to find food. They have been know, when they find a good food source, to build canals from the food source to their pond so they can float the food back to their ponds.

Beavers are **monogamous**, having only one mate. They usually have between two and three kits. The parents care for the kits for up to two years. They have a family hierarchy, in which the female, the matriarch, is in charge. The household will include the mother and father, the yearling kits and the newborn kits. The yearlings assist with the care of the kits as well as the parents, helping provide food and protection.

The kits are born with full fur and their eyes open. They are able to swim within the first 24 hours. After only a couple of days the parents take them out of the lodge for their swim and explore. They are weaned between 2 weeks and up to 90 days. The American Beaver can live up to 24 years.

There are many signs to watch for. The most obvious is a stick dam or lodge. Tree stumps that have been chewed off to a point are another good sign. Fresh signs are also wood shavings and small trails to the water.

The beaver front track measures 2 ½ to 3 7/8 inches in length and 2 ¼ to 3 ½ inches in width (Elbroch, 2003). They are asymmetrical. Toe # 1 is smaller, and toes #3 and #4 point forward while toes #2 and #5 point toward the sides. All toes are curved. Some of the metacarpal pads are fused together. Two additional pads toward the heel at the back of the track may or not be visible. Their nails are long and prominently shown in tracks.

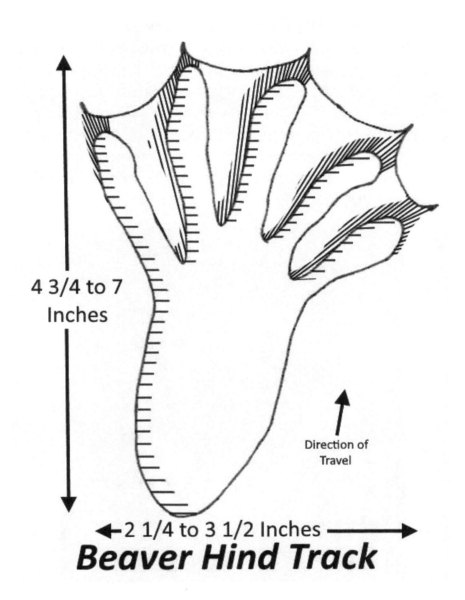

4 3/4 to 7
Inches

Direction of
Travel

←2 1/4 to 3 1/2 Inches →

Beaver Hind Track

The beaver hind track measures 4 ¾ to 7 inches in length, and are 3 ¼ to 5 ¼ inches wide. They have five long toes and the first and second toe are not always shown in the track. They have webs between the toes, which may or may not be visible in the track. The rear paw nails are large, short, and blunt. The toe pads are joined together to make larger pads but they may or may not show. The beaver's walking stride measures 6 to 11 ½ inches in length and 5 ¾ to 11 inches in width. The beaver's bounding stride measures 10 to 32 inches in length and 6 ¾ to 13 ½ inches in width (Elbroch, 2003).

Personal Tracking Record:

Front Track ☐   Hind Track ☐   Scat ☐

Other Sign Found: _____
Date Found: _____
Habitat Found: _____
Place Found: _____
Parent's Initials: _____

Personal Tracking Record:

Front Track ☐   Hind Track ☐   Scat ☐

Other Sign Found: _____
Date Found: _____
Habitat Found: _____
Place Found: _____
Parent's Initials: _____

Personal Tracking Record:

Front Track ☐   Hind Track ☐   Scat ☐

Other Sign Found: _____
Date Found: _____
Habitat Found: _____
Place Found: _____
Parent's Initials: _____

 Hooded Skunk

Mephitis macroura

Don't try this at home kids, he's sitting at the business end of this skunk!!

Wesley, pictured here, is a domesticated hooded skunk with his scent glands removed. Skunks are known for their ability to spray a liquid with a strong odor. This spray is a mixture of sulfur, butane, and methane compounds. They use their spray as a defense. They have two glands on either side of the anus and because of additional muscles, they are able to spray accurately up to 10 feet. This spray can travel up to 15 feet with a mist that can travel up to 30 feet.

In addition to its extreme odor, the spray can be nauseating, and can cause skin irritation and even temporary blindness. It can even ward off bears from attacking. It is used for displays of aggression, threat and fear. When threatened skunks raise their tails, stamp their feet, and perform bluff charges and handstands as warnings. This scent can be detected by the human nose for up to 3 miles. Enough of this musk is stored for five to six shots. The hooded skunk musk is similar to the striped skunk, however, has four added compounds. The skunk musk antidote still works for the hooded skunk musk as well as the striped skunk musk.

Skunk musk antidote (to remove the smell):

- One quart of 3% hydrogen peroxide,
- ¼ cup of baking soda,
- 1 teaspoon of Dawn liquid dishwashing soap

The hooded skunk appears different from the striped skunk with its long tail mixed with black and white hair and longer coat of fur. The hooded skunk has long hair at the back of the neck and head making it appear like a hood. The hooded skunk has 3 different color patterns including a white backed morph with a thick white stripe down their back with a pair of lateral white stripes running down their sides; a black backed morph that is all black with only the white stripes running down it's sides and an all black pattern that does not have any stripes. The hooded skunk is are smaller compared to the striped skunk but larger than the spotted skunk. They measure from 55.8cm to 79cm long and weigh from .88 pound to 5.94 pounds. Skunks have very poor vision and can only see about 10 feet. They have very long claws that help them dig for food or dig burrows.

Hooded Skunk Territory
IUCN Red List (2019)

Hooded skunks are **nocturnal**, primarily active at night. They are primarily solitary until breeding season. They will build a burrow in any protected place with up to five entrances about 8 inches in diameter.

They will also make a den in existing rock ledges and crevices. They will occupy abandoned dens from other animals or find spaces under human buildings. These entrances are well hidden, but they sometimes mark these entrances with nesting materials and snagged hairs. The burrows have one to three chambers about twelve to fifteen inches in diameter, one chamber will have a nest of dried grass. **Maternal dens**, a den where the mother gives birth and nurtures the young, are below ground. While foraging the hooded skunk can be seen moving slowly along rock walls and inconspicuously through or near dense vegetation for cover.

They will breed in early spring. They are **polygynous**, meaning that one male will mate with multiple females. They have three to eight kits. When these kits are born, they are blind and deaf. After three weeks, their eyes will open. They are weaned after two months. They stay with their mother for up to one year until the kits are ready to mate. They will forage together with their mother. The young are know to bite, squeal, stomp their feet, run at, raise their tails at and even spray one another during a fighting bought.

The hooded skunk is an **omnivore**, eating both plants and animals. It is primarily an insectivore, where the majority of it's diet is earwigs, stink bugs and beetles. They also eat small vertebrates, fruits, bird eggs and human garbage. Only one percent of it's diet is plant material, though they do eat prickly pear cactus.

This hooded skunk track measures the front paw 1 5/8 to 1 15/16 inches in length and 15/16 to 1 1/8 inches in width. They have five toes. Toe # 1 is the smallest, located on the inside of the track. The toes do not splay (spread apart). The interdigital pads are fused to make one larger pad. The nails are long and large and usually make marks. There is a heel pad, and a proximal pad, which may or may not show up in the track. The hind foot track measures 1 5/16 to 2 1/8 inches in length and 15/16 to 1 1/8 inches in width.

Again, there are five toes, the smallest does not always show up in the track. The palm pads, interdigital pads, is fused to make one large pad. But the palm and the heel are clearly separate in the track. The nails may or may not show up in the track. These tracks are very similar in size with those of the striped skunk. The skunk's stride measures 5 to 7 ½ inches in length and 3 to 4 ¼ inches in width (Elbroch, 2003).

Hooded Skunk Front Track

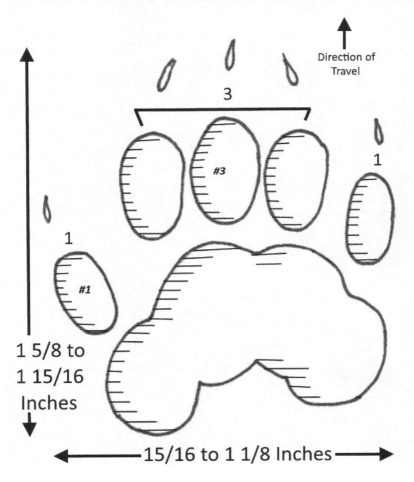

Toe #1 is the smaller inside toe, this shows these are right feet. Toe grouping is a 1 toe, 3 toes, 1 toe pattern showing this is a member of the weasel family.

Hooded Skunk Hind Track

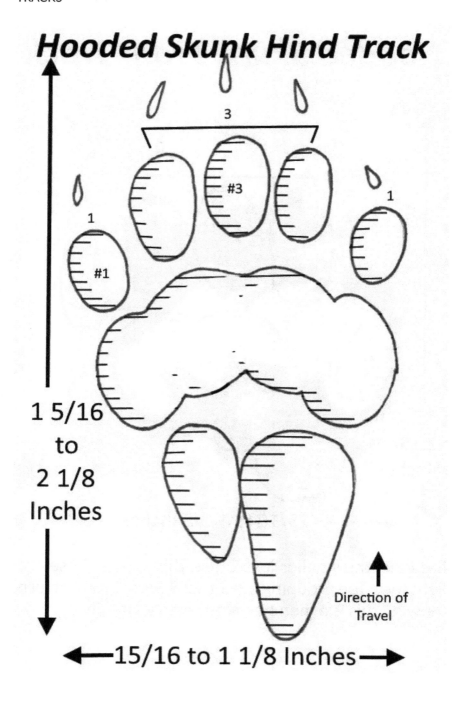

3

#3

1

1

#1

1

1 5/16
to
2 1/8
Inches

Direction of
Travel

←—15/16 to 1 1/8 Inches—→

 Striped Skunk

Mephitis mephitis

This author personally tested the skunk musk antidote after this skunk sprayed her in the process of getting this photograph.
Trust me, the antidote works!!

It may be hard to believe, but, the striped skunk is known for its docile behavior. They will often ignore other animals other than during the breeding season. Skunks are known for their ability to spray a liquid with a strong odor. This spray is a mixture of sulfur, butane, and methane. They use their spray as a defense. They have two glands on either side of the anus and because of additional muscles, they are able to spray accurately up to 10 feet. This spray can travel up to 15 feet with a mist that can travel up to 30 feet. This spray, in addition to its extreme odor, can be nauseating, can cause skin irritation and even temporary blindness. This spray can even ward off bears from attack. This spray is used for displays of aggression, threat and fear. When threatened skunks raise their tails, stamp their feet, perform bluff charges and handstands as warnings. This scent can be detected by the human nose for up to 3 miles. Enough of this musk is stored for five to six shots. If approached the striped skunk will face a potential predator while arching it's back and raising its tail, then stomp the ground with its front legs as a warning. They can perform a handstand if they stomp the ground while backing away and arching their back. Sudden noises or movements can also cause a striped skunk to spray.

The habitat for the striped skunk is a bit different than the hooded skunk. It includes woodlands, forests, wooded ravines, grassy plains, scrubland riparian areas and some urban environments. The striped skunk can be found throughout the continental United States.

Striped Skunk Territory
IUCN Red List (2019)

The striped skunk has primarily black fur. They have a thin white stripe from the top of their snout over their forehead and down the back of their neck. This white strip splits into a V around their shoulders. This V white stripe continues into two white strips on the edges of their bushy black tail. They have a small triangle shaped head with short ears and black eyes. They have stout legs with long foreclaws for digging. There is a little sexual dimorphism with the male being 10% larger than the females. Both males and females measure between 52 and 77 cm in body length. Their front feet have long curved claws adapted for digging, while their claws on the hind feet are shorter and straighter.

They weigh between 4 to 10 pounds. Striped skunks do not hibernate maintaining their regular metabolism. Due to this they use up their body fat stores and loose up to 50% of their body weight.

Females can have a litter from 2 to 10 kits. The kits do not open their eyes for 3 weeks. They are weaned between 6 and 7 weeks. At this age their mother teaches them to forage and hunt. They can be seen walking in a single file line behind their mother during their lessons.

The striped skunk is primarily nocturnal, though some can be crepuscular. During the daytime, the striped skunk den in abandoned underground dens of other animals. They are able to dig their own den if necessary. They will also use hollowed logs, trees, rock or brush piles and any opening to an available building. In cold winter climates, they will change from their above summer ground dens to winter underground dens. They will use these underground dens from fall to early spring. Even though they do not truly hibernate with a change of metabolism, they will become inactive during the winter. During the winter, it is common to see communal denning between females or even females with a single male. They will remain in one winter den throughout the winter, when the warmer weather comes, they may use multiple dens.

The striped skunk is an opportunistic omnivore. It is adaptable and will change it's diet as needed. During the warmer months they are primarily insectivores. They will eat grasshoppers, crickets, beetles, larvae and bees, worms, crayfish, small mammals, eggs and the young of ground nesting birds, amphibians, reptiles, carrion, and fish. Additionally, the striped skunk eats vegetation when in season including corn, nightshade, ground fruits, black and ground cherries.

Striped Skunk Front Track

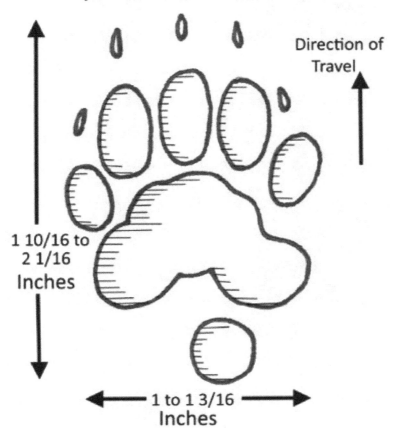

Direction of Travel

1 10/16 to 2 1/16 Inches

1 to 1 3/16 Inches

The striped skunk front track measures 1 10/16 to 2 1/16 inches length and 1 to 1 3/16 inches wide. The front track has five toes. The heel pad may or may not show in the track (Elbroch, 2003).

The striped skunk's hind track measures from 1 5/16 to 2 inches in length and measures 15/16 to 1 3/16 inches in width (Elbroch, 2003).

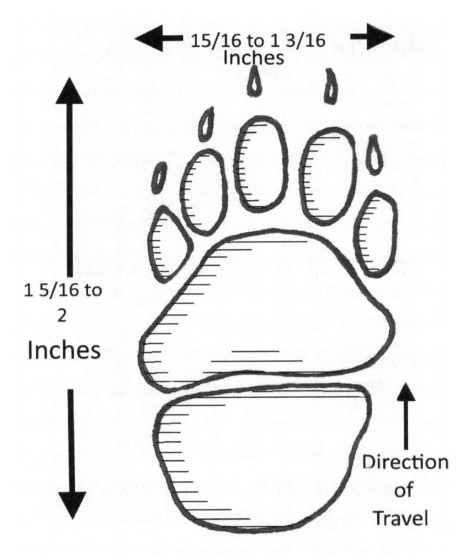

15/16 to 1 3/16 Inches

1 5/16 to 2 Inches

Direction of Travel

Striped Skunk Hind Track

The hind track also has five toes. Toe #1 is the smallest and is not always seen in the tracks.

Personal Tracking Record:

Front Track ☐   Hind Track ☐   Scat ☐

Other Sign Found: _____
Date Found: _____
Habitat Found: _____
Place Found: _____
Parent's Initials: _____

Personal Tracking Record:

Front Track ☐   Hind Track ☐   Scat ☐

Other Sign Found: _____
Date Found: _____
Habitat Found: _____
Place Found: _____
Parent's Initials: _____

Personal Tracking Record:

Front Track ☐   Hind Track ☐   Scat ☐

Other Sign Found: _____
Date Found: _____
Habitat Found: _____
Place Found: _____
Parent's Initials: _____

 Porcupine

Erethizon dorsatum

The New World porcupine can climb trees and lives in a wooded area. They are both **nocturnal**, out at night, and **crepuscular**, out during sunrise and sunset.

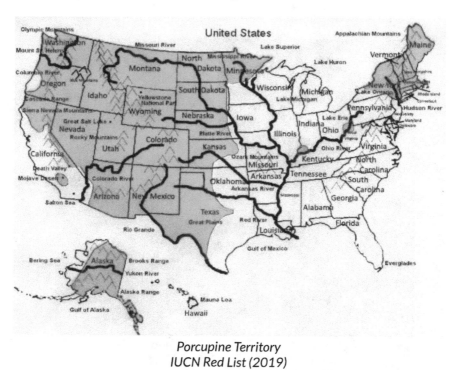

Porcupine Territory
IUCN Red List (2019)

The North American porcupine can reach 33 inches in length and up to 40 pounds. They have sharp quills or spines that protect against predators. Their quills are attached singly rather than grouped in clusters. They are not able to shoot their quills but they are released by contact or may drop out when the porcupine shakes its body. New quills will grow to replace the old ones. The North American porcupine's quills have a barb on them that can get stuck in the flesh of an attacker and are painful to remove. The quills take different forms depending on the species. The quills are modified hairs that are coated with **keratin**, a substance that makes up fingernails, and are embedded in the skin musculature. When a predator gets a quill lodged, the quill's barb acts to pull the quill further into the tissue when the predator has normal muscle movement. This can move the quill several millimeters per day. Due to the quill penetration and subsequent infection, predators have been known to die. The single quills are interspersed with bristles, hair and underfur. These quills are hollow and also assist in insulation in the winter.

These quills are not the only defense that porcupines have. The North American porcupine becomes agitated and releases a strong odor to warn away predators. The smell is described to be similar to human body odor, goats or some cheeses. They will raise their spines and rattle them to warn predators giving them a visual and auditory warning. If the predators continue the porcupine will swing its tail with its quills raised.

They spend much of their time in trees. Porcupines are herbivores and will eat leaves, bark, herbs, twigs, green plants, roots, stems, and berries. In the winter they may eat tree bark. A porcupine will have separate trees for resting and eating. This is the third largest rodent. They are large, rounded and slow. Porcupines are dark brown or black in color with white accents. They have a stocky body, a small face, short legs and a short tail. They are the longest-lived rodent and living up to 27 years. Porcupines have antibiotics in their skin that prevent infection when it sustains damage from its own quills from falling out of trees. They tend to fall out of trees because they prefer the tender buds and twigs at the ends of the tree branches.

North American porcupines have multiple adaptations for tree climbing. They have long claws, five in the front with a vestigial thumb. Additionally, they have palms and soles of their feet that are naked with pebbly skin. This skin has a finely developed sense of touch. These adaptations greatly assist in navigating at night. They use their claws and specially adapted soles to easily climb large trunks and minute branches. These claws and soles allow the porcupine to hold onto the tree with it's hind limbs while using its front limbs to aid in feeding. Lastly, the porcupine uses the quills on the tail to stab the tree to additionally anchor the animal in the tree.

The North American porcupine can be found in tropical and temperate parts of America. They live in coniferous and mixed forests, and deserts on rocky outcrops and hillsides. They have adapted to tundra and deserts. Porcupines are nearsighted and slow moving. They do not hibernate, but sleep in and stay close to their dens during winter.

Did you know?
Porcupines have a second
defense? They secrete a musk
something akin to body odor.

During the fall season the female will secrete a thick mucus that mixes with her urine and creates a smell that attracts males. She will also use high pitched vocalizations to attract a mate. Males will compete to assert dominance in order to breed. They will compete while in trees using high pitched vocalizations, violent biting and using their quills as weapons. Once attracted, the males will sit below the female in the same tree. Later the male will approach the female and spray her with his urine. This causes a hormone reaction that allows the female to become ready for breeding. While breeding, one the ground both porcupines tighten their skin to keep their quills flat so they are not injured.

The female will give birth to a single young after a 210 day pregnancy. The newborn's quills will harden soon after birth. Mother porcupines will not defend their young but will provide all the maternal care. During the daytime, the mother will hide her young on the ground, she will then sleep in the tree above her young. They will nurse for up to four months. During this time, the newborns learn to climb trees and forage. The young will become independent at five months and will spend their first winter on their own.

The porcupine's front track measures 2 ¼ to 3 3/8 inches long and 1 ¼ to 1 7/8 inches wide. They have four very long toes. Toe #1 does not show in the tracks. The other toes appear to curve inward. Toe pads do not show up.

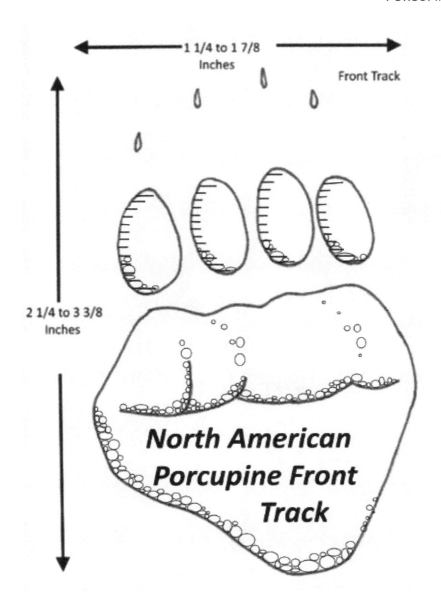

1 1/4 to 1 7/8 Inches

Front Track

2 1/4 to 3 3/8 Inches

North American Porcupine Front Track

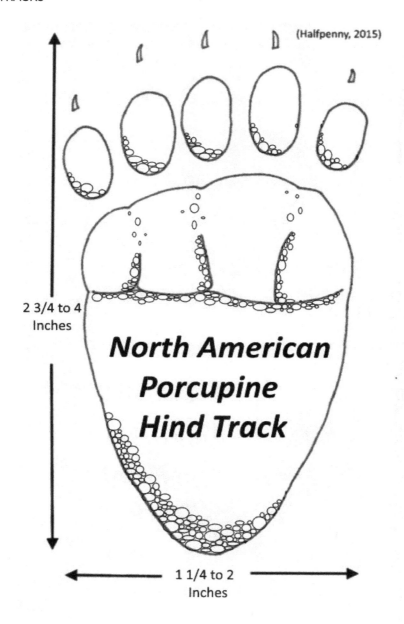

(Halfpenny, 2015)

2 3/4 to 4
Inches

North American Porcupine Hind Track

1 1/4 to 2
Inches

Their hind tracks are slightly larger than the front tracks and measure 2 ¾ inches to 4 inches long and 1 ¼ to 2 inches wide (Elbroch, 2003). For both tracks look for claw marks in front of the palm some distance.

In the tree on the right, you can see that a porcupine has climbed up and eaten the bark, leaving the lower bark intact.

Personal Tracking Record:

Front Track ☐   Hind Track ☐   Scat ☐

Other Sign Found: _____
Date Found: _____
Habitat Found: _____
Place Found: _____
Parent's Initials: _____

Personal Tracking Record:

Front Track ☐   Hind Track ☐   Scat ☐

Other Sign Found: _____
Date Found: _____
Habitat Found: _____
Place Found: _____
Parent's Initials: _____

Personal Tracking Record:

Front Track ☐   Hind Track ☐   Scat ☐

Other Sign Found: _____
Date Found: _____
Habitat Found: _____
Place Found: _____
Parent's Initials: _____

 Northern River Otter

Lontra canadensis

The North American river otter can vary in size from 16 inches up to 48 inches. They can weigh from 11 pounds up to 66 pounds. They are brown in color with a lighter brown on the chest, throat, and underside of the belly. They have specialized fur with a dense underfur that can have about 70,000 hairs per square centimeter. They also have long guard hairs that trap a layer of insulating air while they are under water. The otter has a long thin muscular body built for vigorous swimming. They have short legs with webbed paws. Their tail is thick at the base and tapers down to a point and is covered with the same fur. They have stiff long whiskers called **vibrissae** around the nose and snout. These whiskers are extremely sensitive and are used to locate food even under water. They have tufts of fur on their elbows. Their ears are small and round and are able to close under the water. They also close their nose when diving as well.

American River Otter Territory
IUCN Red List (2019)

Otters mainly eat fish but also catch frogs, cray fish, and crabs as well as birds, some eggs and small mammals. Otters spend the majority of their time foraging in the water but also devote much of their time to resting on land. They have an unusually high metabolism to meet the special demands of their watery habitat.

This requires them to eat 15 % of their body weight per day in fish. Otters live up to 25 years.

The habitat of males is different than that of females. Males spend most of their time in larger rivers and along the seacoast. Female otters's habitat is usually in smaller streams and in sheltered bays. Females ranges can be up to 25 miles while male's habitats are around 52 miles. Males and females only briefly associate during the mating season. The male otters take no part in raising their young. Males may live in bachelor group of up to 12 individuals. Females give birth to up to five pups. They teach the pups to swim. Pups only dive after they are two months old. Mothers will then teach the pups to fish by catching fish and releasing them for the pups to go after.

Pups are born blind and helpless but with fur. Their eyes open after one month and they are weaned at three months. They leave at six months.

Otters can be very playful sliding down mud slides or diving through snow drifts. The juveniles may rough play tumbling along the shore or chase each other into the water. These play activities serve a purpose strengthening social bonds, practicing hunting techniques and scent marking. North American River Otters have scent glands near the base of their tails that they will use to mark on vegetation in their home range. They will also mark with urine and feces.

Additionally, they will communicate through body posture and other body signals.

The lope stride measures 15 to 40 inches in length. The width of the trail measures 4 ½ to 7 inches wide.

The width of the slide trail measures 6 to 10 inches long. This is when the otters go sliding on their tummies down a slope on the snow or mud.

The Northern River Otter's front track measures 2 1/8 to 3 1/3 inches in length and 1 7/8 to 3 inches wide (Elbroch, 2003). The tracks show they have five toes. Toe # 1 is the smallest. Webbing may or may not show in the track. The palm pad is lobed and fused. There is an additional pad at the heel that may or may not show. The front track is more symmetrical than the rear track but is smaller. The hind track measures 2 1/8 to 4 inches in length and 2 1/8 to

3 ¾ inches wide (Elbroch, 2003). Toe #1 is well developed and long. Hind tracks are larger than the front. Toe #1 sits back farther.

River Otter Front Track

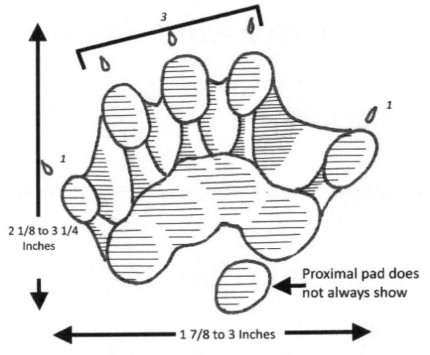

3

1

1

2 1/8 to 3 1/4 Inches

Proximal pad does not always show

◀— 1 7/8 to 3 Inches —▶

It can be difficult to tell the difference between otter tracks and fisher tracks. Otters are very social and may have tracks of multiple animals while fishers are territorial and solitary. The otter's rear track is larger than their front track and more obviously webbed than the front track. The fisher has dense fur on the bottom of its feet while the otter has very sparse fur on its feet. The size of the otter's toe #1 on the rear track is equal to the other toes. Toe one is long and sticks out while a fishers' toe #1 is the smallest or absent in tracks.

River Otter Hind Track

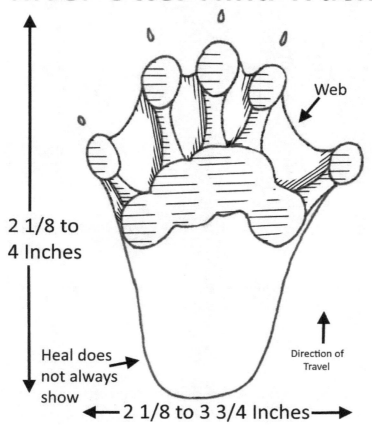

Web

2 1/8 to
4 Inches

Heal does
not always
show

Direction of
Travel

←— 2 1/8 to 3 3/4 Inches —→

Notice the 1 toe, 3 toes, 1 toe pattern again. This shows the river otter is part of the weasel family. The inter-digital pad also has a chevron shape. The heel does not always show on the hind track. There usually is pretty obvious webbing between the toes.

Personal Tracking Record:

Front Track ☐   Hind Track ☐   Scat ☐

Other Sign Found: _____

Date Found: _____

Habitat Found: _____

Place Found: _____

Parent's Initials: _____

Personal Tracking Record:

Front Track ☐   Hind Track ☐   Scat ☐

Other Sign Found: _____

Date Found: _____

Habitat Found: _____

Place Found: _____

Parent's Initials: _____

Personal Tracking Record:

Front Track ☐   Hind Track ☐   Scat ☐

Other Sign Found: _____

Date Found: _____

Habitat Found: _____

Place Found: _____

Parent's Initials: _____

 Raccoon

Procyon lotor

The Raccoon has a fox like face with a black mask across the eyes, gray fur, and a ringed tail. The black mask is believed to assist in reducing glare, helping with their night vision. Their long stiff guard hairs, which are usually gray, assists in shedding moisture. This guard hair is usually shades of gray and occasionally is brown. They weigh between 11 and 18 pounds and measure 16 to 28 inches long with an added 10 inches for their tail. The males are 20 to 30 percent larger than females. During the beginning of winter, a raccoon will weigh twice as much as they will in spring due to fat storage for the winter. During the winter it does not hibernate, the raccoon's metabolic rate remains constant, thus causing them to burn through their fat stores.

Raccoon Territory
IUCN Red List (2019)

The raccoon is able to stand on its hind legs in order to examine objects with its front paws. The raccoon's front paws are able to identify objects before touching them with the **vibrissae** hairs that are located above their sharp non-retractable claws. Their hypersensitive front paws are protected by a thin horny layer that becomes pliable when wet. The most important sense for a raccoon is its sense of touch. The raccoon's dexterous front paws are seen rubbing, dunking and manipulating their food. This is not hand washing but is what they do to find aquatic prey like crayfish as well as helping soften the horny skin on their fingers to help them feel their food. Raccoon are also able to rotate their hind feet so they can point backwards enabling them to climb down a tree headfirst.

Raccoons are almost completely color-blind but can see some green colors. They have poor long-distance vision. Their sense of smell helps them find their way in the dark and is important for communication with other raccoons. They have anal glands they use for marking along with urine and scat. They have extraordinary hearing and are able to hear quiet noises like earthworms moving.

Raccoons are generally nocturnal and most active between sunset and midnight. They are omnivores and will forage at night, preferably near lakes, streams or marshy areas. In the spring, their diet is mainly insects, worms and animals that are available early in the year. The raccoon prefers fruits and nuts which are available in late summer and autumn and help build up the needed fat for winter. Raccoons only occasionally eat larger prey such as birds and mammals but prefer prey that is easier to catch especially fish, amphibians and bird eggs.

Raccoon's mating is triggered by increasing daylight between January and mid-March. They are **polygynous** meaning they will mate with multiple partners. The female will give birth to between 4 and 6 kits. The kits are born blind and deaf at birth. Once the kits weigh about 2 pounds they begin to leave the den and explore. They begin eating solid food between 6 and 9 weeks old. They are usually weaned by 16 weeks. During the fall, after their mother has shown them dens and taught them feeding grounds, the kits split up. The females kits will stay close to their mother while the males will move up to 12 miles away.

Raccoons depend on climbing higher up when they are threatened. Due to this, they tend to avoid open terrain. Raccoons prefer tree hollows and rock crevices for dens, however they will use abandoned burrows, caves, mines deserted buildings, barns, garages, houses and dense undergrowth. The preferable habitat is deciduous forests or mixed forests with water or marshes. They require access to water.

The raccoon gate is a shuffle gate, however, the raccoon's top running speed is between 10 and 15 miles per hour. They are also able to swim with an average speed of 3 miles per hours and they can stay in water for several hours. They are fairly agile swimmers considering that they do not have any webbing between their fingers.

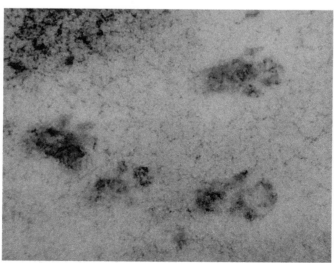

Because the hind feet are in front of the front feet in the snow, we know this raccoon was loping

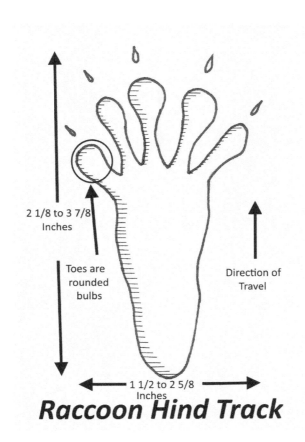

2 1/8 to 3 7/8
Inches

Toes are
rounded
bulbs

Direction of
Travel

1 1/2 to 2 5/8
Inches

Raccoon Hind Track

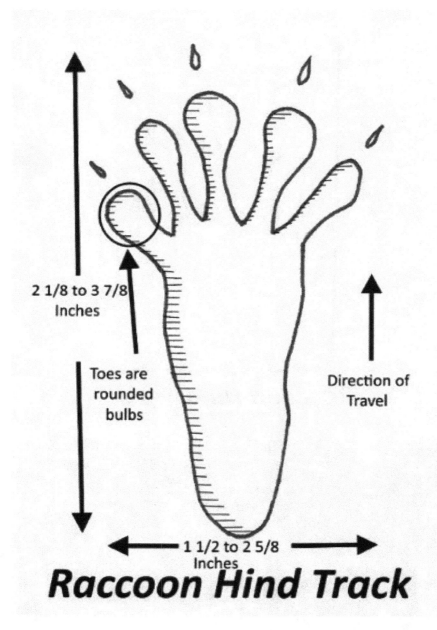

2 1/8 to 3 7/8 Inches

Toes are rounded bulbs

Direction of Travel

1 1/2 to 2 5/8 Inches

Raccoon Hind Track

Raccoon scat

Personal Tracking Record:

Front Track ☐   Hind Track ☐   Scat ☐

Other Sign Found: _____
Date Found: _____
Habitat Found: _____
Place Found: _____
Parent's Initials: _____

Personal Tracking Record:

Front Track ☐   Hind Track ☐   Scat ☐

Other Sign Found: _____
Date Found: _____
Habitat Found: _____
Place Found: _____
Parent's Initials: _____

Personal Tracking Record:

Front Track ☐   Hind Track ☐   Scat ☐

Other Sign Found: _____
Date Found: _____
Habitat Found: _____
Place Found: _____
Parent's Initials: _____

 North American Badger

Taxidea taxus

The North American badger is found in the northern, western, and central United States, northern Mexico and south central Canada west to a few areas in southwestern British Columbia. Their preferred habitat is open grasslands with available prey. The North American badger prefers prairies with sandy loam soils where it can dig easily. They are most commonly found in treeless areas including tall grass, short grass prairies, grass-dominated meadows and fields within forest habitats and shrub steppe communities.

American Badger Territory
IUCN Red List (2019)

The North American Badger has a wide flattened body with short muscular legs that averages between 1 ½ to 2 feet long with a 4 to 6 inch tail. They weight between 8 to 25 pounds. They have a white stripe that extends from their nose over it's head, down between it's shoulders. Some southern species this white stripe extends all the way to the tail. They have a shaggy coat with a triangle shaped head, small ears and powerful jaws. They have long front claws up to 2 inches long. They have very good vision, sensitive smell and hearing. They have a scent gland that produces a strong musky odor they use as a defense when threatened. The North American badger tends to be very clean like a cat and will bury it's scat and regularly groom it's fur.

Badgers are normally a solitary animal but will expand their territory for mating season. Mating season occurs in late summer or early fall. The embryos will not implant for several months until winter. Some males will mate with multiple females. The female is only pregnant for 6 weeks. The female will raise her young alone. She will prepare an elaborate burrow digging 10 feet below the surface for 30 or more feet in multiple passageways. The nursery burrow is lined with dried grass. Litters ranging from one to five but averaging three are born from late March to early April. North American badgers are born blind, with light fur and helpless. Their eyes open between 4 and 6 weeks. The mothers will feed their young solid food before they wean them. The mother will continue to feed them solid food for two or three months after they are weaned. The young come out of the dens on their own at 5 to 6 weeks once their eyes are open. These families will break up and the juveniles disperse from the end of June to August. Most females will become pregnant for the first time when they are a year old. The males usually don't mate until they are two years old. Their average life span is 9 to 10 years.

The North American badger den is an enlarged gopher and other prey hole. Their dens range from 4 to 10 feet deep and 4 to 6 feet wide. A female badger may create two to four burrows in close proximity with a connecting tunnel for safety for her young. A mound of dirt from digging out the burrow usually appears in front of the burrow entrance. They will even carry some sticks to help hide their entrance. The entrance can also often be hidden beneath a log or a bush. A view from a distance reveals a mound-like roof of the burrow.

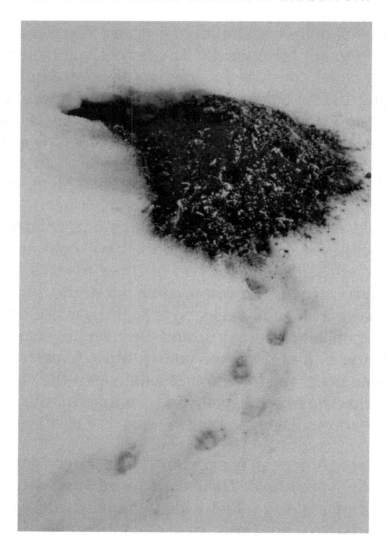

The North American badger is typically nocturnal, but in some remote areas they will occasionally come out during the daytime. Some females will hunt during the day to feed their young. They are excellent hunters and are known to block the exit hole before going after their prey. They are very fast diggers and can run relatively fast. The North American badger is a carnivore that usually preys on mice, squirrels, prairie dogs and groundhogs. They have also been known to eat rattle snakes. They were previously thought to be immune to the snake venom; however, it has been found that their fur is so thick that the rattle-snake cannot bite through it, and thus protects the badger.

The North American badger front track measures 2 7/8 to 3 7/8 inches long and 1 9/16 to 2 5/8 wide (Elbroch, 2003). It has five toes. Toe #1 is the smallest and does not always show up. The palm pad, the inter-digital pad, is fused into one large pad that is wider than it is long. They have long nails that usually show up. The front track is larger than the hind track.

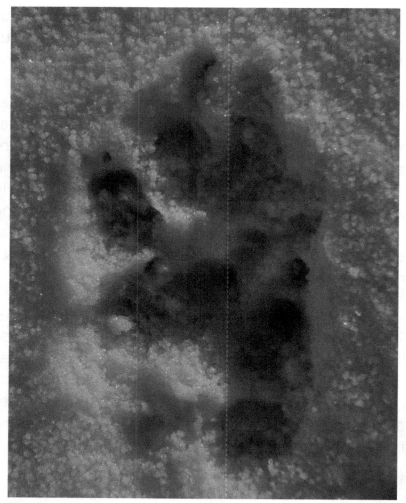

Here is a double track where the rear foot stepped in the front foot track, more likely indicating he was trotting

The hind track measures 1 7/8 to 2 ¾ inches long and 1 3/8 to 2 inches wide. The walking stride measures 5 ½ to 9 ¾ inches. The trotting stride measures 10 to 15 inches. The loping stride measures 10 to 12 inches (Elbroch, 2003).

The North American badger will walk while foraging, often travel at a trot, and will lope when alarmed. They do not climb. They are solitary animals so there will only be one set of tracks.

Notice in these drawings the middle three toes are grouped closer together in a 1 toe, 3 toes, 1 toe pattern. This indicates that this animal is part of the weasel family. Toe #3 is the largest. Toe #1 is the smallest on the inside of the track. These sketches show the right track.

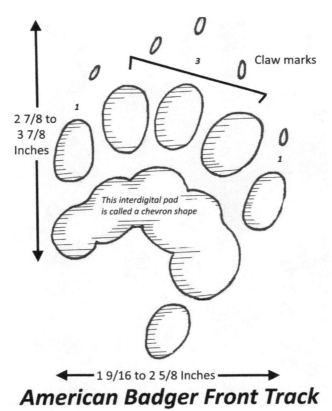

2 7/8 to 3 7/8 Inches

Claw marks

This interdigital pad is called a chevron shape

1 9/16 to 2 5/8 Inches

American Badger Front Track

There has been debate about whether badgers and coyotes at times have a symbiotic relationship. Coyotes will take advantage when badgers pursue their prey down a burrow and the prey gets out the escape exit and will grab it before the badger can. Is this taking advantage by the coyote or working together? Here are a couple pictures of the symbiotic relationship where the coyote and badger worked together to distract the mother antelope by getting her to chase the coyote, while the badger searched for her new baby so the badger and coyote could share lunch.

Personal Tracking Record:

Front Track ☐   Hind Track ☐   Scat ☐

Other Sign Found: _____

Date Found: _____

Habitat Found: _____

Place Found: _____

Parent's Initials: _____

Personal Tracking Record:

Front Track ☐   Hind Track ☐   Scat ☐

Other Sign Found: _____

Date Found: _____

Habitat Found: _____

Place Found: _____

Parent's Initials: _____

Personal Tracking Record:

Front Track ☐   Hind Track ☐   Scat ☐

Other Sign Found: _____

Date Found: _____

Habitat Found: _____

Place Found: _____

Parent's Initials: _____

 Virginia Opossum

Didelphis virginiana

The opossum (Virginia opossum) is the only true **marsupial** in North America. Marsupials are animals in which the females have a pouch to carry their young in. They live in both trees and on the ground- **semi-arboreal**. They have a long snout with 50 teeth, which is a great deal of teeth for a mammal. The Virginia opossum are medium sized, with pointed snouts and hairless tail, hands, and feet. They have gray or white fur with a white snout and round dark eyes. Opossums have a naked tail with has **scutes** on it, a kind of armored scale. This amazing tail is also **prehensile**- meaning it can also hold onto and grasp items. Opossums will carry nesting material as well as their young with these tails.

Virginia Opossum Territory
IUCN (2019)

Their coloration may vary based on the climate they habitat. Northern populations have lighter guard hairs, thicker underfur and appear more grizzled. Southern populations have thinner underfur which makes them appear darker. Their furless tails and ears are susceptible to frostbite. The full-grown males, jacks, are slightly larger than the female, jills, and have larger canine teeth.

Opossums are opportunistic omnivores. They will eat dead animals, insects, rodents, frogs, plants, fruits, grain, eggs and birds. They have teeth that can eat through the skeletal remains of rodents and roadkill. Opossums are estimated to eat about 5000 ticks a year and are believed to reduce the amount of Lyme disease. Opossums are also known to eat venomous snakes. They have an immunity to most snake venom. Due to their exceptionally varied diet, opossums are able to survive in a wide range of habitat. Additionally, their low body temperature makes them resistant to rabies.

Opossums can be found in wooded areas and swamp lands. They prefer areas near a water source. They live in woodlands and thickets but are found in human structures for shelter. The Virginia opossum has been moving north in recent years, likely due to climate changes. Opossum will use abandoned dens from other animals as well as tree holes. They will not dig their own dens. They change their denning sites frequently. They will fill their dens with dry leaves or other dry substrate. The females will stay with the same den longer while her joeys have left her pouch but have not completely weaned yet. Their habitat is restricted by temperature and snow depth. They do not hibernate.

The opossum's front track measures between 1 and 2 5/16 inches in length and 1 1/4 to 2 1/2 inches wide.

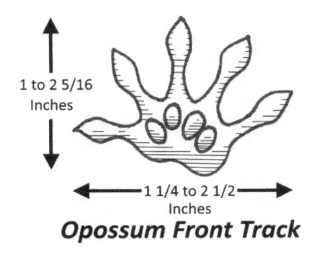

1 to 2 5/16
Inches

←——— 1 1/4 to 2 1/2 ——→
Inches

Opossum Front Track

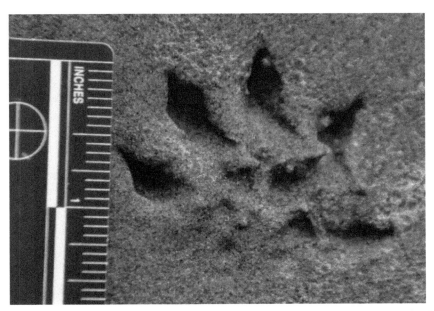

The opossum's rear track measures between 1 3/16 and 2 3/4 inches in length and 1 1/2 to 3 inches wide.

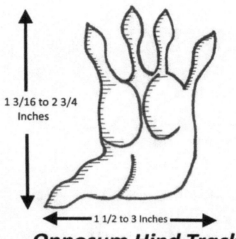

1 3/16 to 2 3/4
Inches

1 1/2 to 3 Inches

Opposum Hind Track

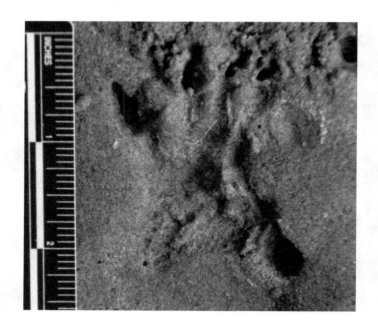

The Virginia opossum averages only one litter per year of 8 to 13 babies, called **joeys**, however in warmer climates they may have up to 3 litters in a year.

After the joeys emerge from their mother's pouch, they stay with their mother riding on her back while she is foraging for food or they stay in her den. They are able to start eating solid food around 85 days old. They are usually weaned between 93 to 105 days. After they are weaned the joeys become independent. Some will stay in the den with their mother until they reach around 120 days old. The males do not provide any parental care.

Virginia opossum are solitary. Once they have mated they will return to being solitary. Males will have aggressive encounters where they lash their tails and reach at each-other with their front feet. When threatened or harmed, they will play dead. This response is involuntary, they cannot control it. When playing dead, the opossum's eyes are closed or half closed, they can form foaming saliva around the mouth, and their anal glands secrete a foul-smelling fluid. It can take a few minutes to four hours for the opossum to regain consciousness.

Personal Tracking Record:

Front Track ☐   Hind Track ☐   Scat ☐

Other Sign Found: _____

Date Found: _____

Habitat Found: _____

Place Found: _____

Parent's Initials: _____

Personal Tracking Record:

Front Track ☐   Hind Track ☐   Scat ☐

Other Sign Found: _____

Date Found: _____

Habitat Found: _____

Place Found: _____

Parent's Initials: _____

Personal Tracking Record:

Front Track ☐   Hind Track ☐   Scat ☐

Other Sign Found: _____

Date Found: _____

Habitat Found: _____

Place Found: _____

Parent's Initials: _____

 Black-Tailed Prairie Dog

Cynomys ludovicianus

Black tailed prairie dogs are a small brown rodent that measures between 12 and 16 inches long and weighs between 1 and 3 pounds. Females live up to 8 years and males will live up to 5 years and are capable of running up to 35 miles per hour for short distances. Their habitat is in open grassland areas. The prairie dog is a **keystone species** as they serve as vital food source for a number of predators. They are the primary food source for the black-footed ferret, swift fox, golden eagle, American badger and ferruginous hawk and 131 other predators. Their burrows also become homes for other animals including the jack rabbits, toads, and rattle snakes.

Black Tailed Prairie Dog
IUCN Red List (2019)

Black-tailed prairie dogs create extensive underground tunnel systems with designated chambers for sleeping, food storage, nurseries and toileting. The tunnels are interconnected with multiple exit or escape tunnels. These burrows also help with controlling their body temperatures protect from floods, blizzards, prairie fires, etc. The black-tailed prairie dog will cut down all vegetation to six inches around their burrows, allowing them to better see predators. The entrance of the burrow is mounded to keep the burrows from flooding. The nesting chamber is lined with dry grass and is near the bottom of the burrow. The black-tailed prairie dog builds listening chambers near the entrance so they may listen for predators prior to exiting.

Black-tailed prairie dogs live in family groups called **coteries**. These groups include a male, several females and their offspring. They greet other members of the family with nuzzles. The family also interacts through oral contact or kissing and grooming one another. They do not do this with individuals that are outside the family group. The family shares food gathering responsibilities. Although they do eat some insects, they are typically herbivores, subsisting on grasses, seeds, broadleaf forbes, roots, fruit, and buds. Family groups may form wards, and several wards form a prairie dog town. Wards are separated by physical barriers like rocks or trees. Prairie dogs have an extensive communication system warning all the others in the town of predators.

Scientists have discovered that the black-tailed prairie dog has a vocabulary that is more advanced than any other animal language that has been decoded. Research reveals that their language can give incredibly descriptive details including not only that there is a predator approaching, but the size and color of the predator. A jump-yip with a strange arch of the back followed by the shrill yip communicates when a predator leaves the area or can be used in territorial displays.

Prairie dogs will sit up on their hind feet to check out their surroundings. They are very skittish and easily frightened. You can see we scared the pee out of this one

The front track of the prairie dog measures between 1 ¼ and 1 7/8 inches in length and 1 and 1 ½ inches in width. They have five toes. Toe #1 is a thumb. There are three interdigital pads that are fused into one. There are two additional pads at the heel that may or may not show. The nails are long and prominent in the tracks. The front and hind tracks are similar in size. The hind track measures 1 3/8 to 2 ¼ inches in length and 1 to 1 7/16 inches in width. The trail walking stride measures 4 to 6 inches in length and 3 to 4 ½ inches in width. The bound stride measures 9 to 20 inches in length and the width measures 3 ¼ to 4 ¼ inches (Elbroch, 2003).

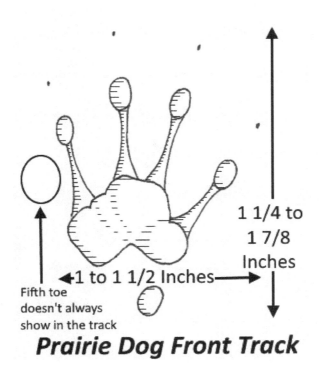

1 1/4 to 1 7/8 Inches

1 to 1 1/2 Inches

Fifth toe doesn't always show in the track

Prairie Dog Front Track

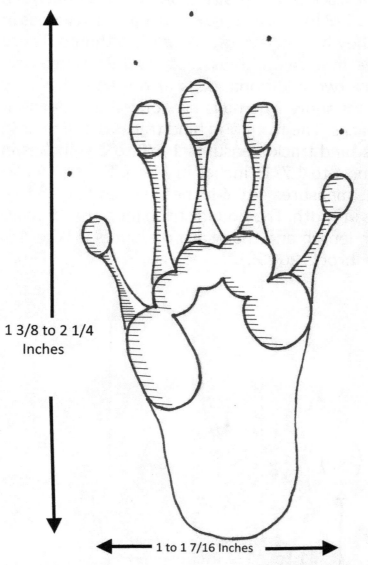

1 3/8 to 2 1/4
Inches

← 1 to 1 7/16 Inches →

Prairie Dog Hind Track

(Elbroch, 2003)

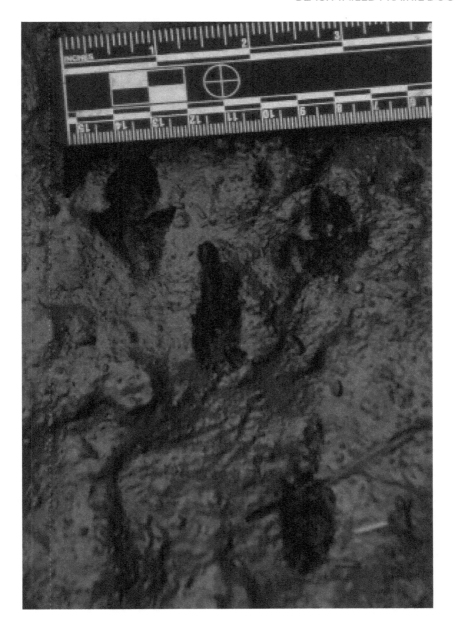

Personal Tracking Record:

Front Track ☐   Hind Track ☐   Scat ☐

Other Sign Found: _____

Date Found: _____

Habitat Found: _____

Place Found: _____

Parent's Initials: _____

Personal Tracking Record:

Front Track ☐   Hind Track ☐   Scat ☐

Other Sign Found: _____

Date Found: _____

Habitat Found: _____

Place Found: _____

Parent's Initials: _____

Personal Tracking Record:

Front Track ☐   Hind Track ☐   Scat ☐

Other Sign Found: _____

Date Found: _____

Habitat Found: _____

Place Found: _____

Parent's Initials: _____

 Least Chipmunk

Tamias minimus

Chipmunks are primarily found in North America. There are 25 species of chipmunks. Least chipmunks are the smallest of the chipmunks weighing between 32 and 50 grahams, or around as much as a regular-size Hershey's chocolate bar. They measure between 185 to 216 millimeters. Chipmunks can be distinguished from other ground squirrels by the striping through their eyes. Chipmunks eye striping runs all the way through their eyes. The least chipmunk have 3 dark stripes and two light stripes on their face, with five dark and 4 light stripes on the sides of their body. They live between 3.5 to 4 years.

Chipmunk Territory
IUCN Red List (2019)

Chipmunks collect and store food for the winter. Least chipmunks are **omnivores**, eating both plant and animals, their diet consists of nuts berries, fruits, grasses, fungi, snails, earthworms, insects and possibly some small mammals and birds. They primarily forage on the ground but they do climb trees for nuts and acorns. However, they are also considered opportunistic predators. During the autumn, they begin storing **non-perishable** foods for winter, food that will not rot. They primarily store their cache of food in large burrows and will remain in these nests until spring. They have large cheek pouches to carry food to their burrows. They have sensitive whiskers on their muzzle on their feet and outside legs.

Least Chipmunks will dig their own burrows with chambers. Others will make their homes in nests, in bushes, or in logs as a summer home but return to underground burrows for the winter. They are usually solitary until mating season. They are **diurnal**, out during daytime. Due to chipmunks storing their food for winter in underground burrows they play a crucial role in dispersing plants and fungi spores including truffles. Beginning in April through the month of October, the majority of the least chipmunk's time is spent foraging. They have cheek pouches that expand allowing the chipmunk to carry multiple items back to their food cache.

The female will choose or construct her nursery nest while she is pregnant. These nursery nests are in underground burrows, located under logs, in stumps, in brush piles or rock piles. There is the nursery chamber but it is connected to additional chambers with cashed food supplies. The nests are lined with grass. The female will choose her nest so it is protected from rainfall and runoff.

Least Chipmunks mate early in the spring and have 2 to 6 young a year. The mother is pregnant, **gestation,** for about 30 days. The newborns are born naked and pink. They do not open their eyes for 28 days. They will have full fur at 40 days. The young emerge from the burrow after about 6 weeks and strike out on their own within a total of 8 weeks from birth. The young begin at 8 weeks gathering their own food for winter.

Least chipmunks will climb trees to sun themselves in cold weather. They are also territorial and will defend their nests and cache sites from intruders. They use visual signs, like body posture, to communicate their territory. They also use a variety of chirps and chatters to communicate their territory, find mates and give warning when they are threatened.

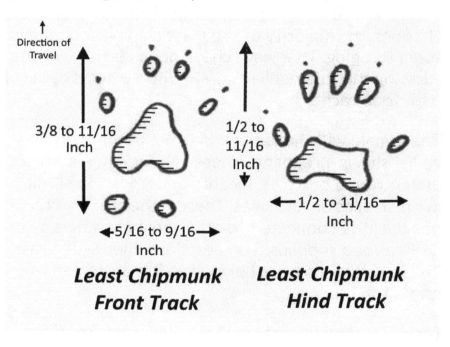

Least Chipmunk Front Track

Least Chipmunk Hind Track

The front track of the least chipmunk measures 3/8 to 11/16 inch in length and 5/16 to 9/16 inches wide. They have 5 toes. Toe # 1 rarely shows up in a track. The palm pads, interdigital pads, are fused into one. There are two additional heel pads at the back edge of the track. The negative space has no fur. Their nails usually show up in the tracks. The hind track measures ½ to 11/16 inch in length and 1/2 to 11/16 inches wide (Elbroch, 2003).

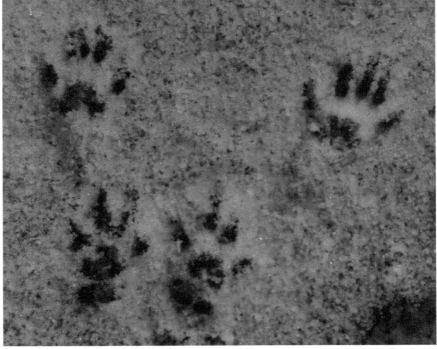

This chipmunk was bounding, moving fast. Its front feet are found behind the hind feet. The hind feet are spread further apart showing they had to move around the front feet.

Chipmunk scat

The scat of the least chipmunk 0.2 to 0.5 centimeters long and resemble a pellet shape found in a small group instead of individual pellets.

Personal Tracking Record:

Front Track ☐   Hind Track ☐   Scat ☐

Other Sign Found: _____

Date Found: _____

Habitat Found: _____

Place Found: _____

Parent's Initials: _____

Personal Tracking Record:

Front Track ☐   Hind Track ☐   Scat ☐

Other Sign Found: _____

Date Found: _____

Habitat Found: _____

Place Found: _____

Parent's Initials: _____

Personal Tracking Record:

Front Track ☐   Hind Track ☐   Scat ☐

Other Sign Found: _____

Date Found: _____

Habitat Found: _____

Place Found: _____

Parent's Initials: _____

 Fox Squirrel

Sciurus niger

*This is a Fox Squirrel often mistaken for a Red Squirrel
or an Eastern Gray Squirrel*

Fox squirrels generally have slender bodies with bushy tails and large eyes. Their hind legs are longer than their front legs. Their color varies. The fox squirrel measures between 17.7 and 27.6 inches, and their tails measure between 7.9 and 13 inches. Their weight ranges between 1.1 and 2.2 pounds. Their large eyes are placed on the sides of their head for a wider field of vision, they also have large ears. They have touch sensitive whiskers called vibrissae on their face above and below their eyes, on their chin and nose, feet, and outside of their legs and forearms. Squirrels have a pair of chisel-shaped incisors in each jaw, and a large gap in front of their premolars with no canine teeth. These incisors grow continuously and get worn down by use. Their other teeth have abrasive chewing surfaces.

Fox Squirrel Territory
IUCN Red List (2019)

Fox squirrels have sharp claws on all of their toes and can climb trees. They have less muscular forelimbs. They are able to descend a tree headfirst by turning their hind legs backwards to use their hind toes as hooks. Their long bushy tails are used to balance, use as a rudder for direction when they jump, as a flag to communicate social signals and as a blanket when sleeping. They also have soft pads on the soles of their feet that help grip on climbing surfaces and on food.

When eating they squat on their hind legs and hold their food in their forepaws. Fox squirrels eat nuts, seeds, fruit, buds, sap and some fungi. They are omnivores and will also eat insects, bird eggs, chicks and small vertebrates. They are considered opportunistic predators. Most squirrels get their water from the plants they digest. They store seeds and nuts for winter. Fox squirrels spread their cache and bury them to prevent other animals or squirrels from stealing. They can bury hundreds of nuts in a season. They can smell nuts 12 feet below the ground surface.

They molt two times a year. For the summer they have soft fine hair and later they get a stiff thick winter coat. Males and females look the same. They only live between 2 and 3 years.

Fox squirrel's primary habitat is in trees. They are very fast and agile using trees to escape predators both on the ground and flying predators. They use the cover from the trees as a refuge.

Where hollow trees are available they are the preferred den site and nurseries. If the hollow log is not available, then the females will create a nest out of leaves outside on a branch. These nests are composed of twigs and leaves. The nesting supplies is usually cut from the tree in which the nest is being built. These nests are roughly globular measuring 30 to 50 cm in diameter with an inner cavity measuring 15 to 20 cm. Older females can breed 2 times a year, whereas the yearling female will only breed once a year. Males do not help with raising the young.

Females can begin having litters at the age of 1 year. Males will mate with multiple females. They will have one litter in the spring between one and six pups. Squirrels warn away intruders by screeching and making rattling calls. If the intruder continues to invade the territory, then they will resort to chasing and physical combat. This territorial defense gets the most intense close to where their food cache is hidden. They use scent marking to communicate among fox squirrels. Fox squirrels will stand upright flicking its tail over their back as a threat to another squirrel.

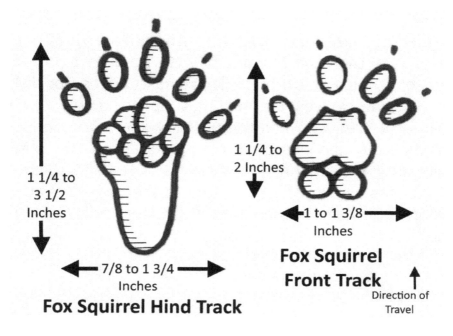

1 1/4 to 2 Inches

1 1/4 to 3 1/2 Inches

1 to 1 3/8 Inches

Fox Squirrel Front Track

Direction of Travel

7/8 to 1 3/4 Inches

Fox Squirrel Hind Track

The front track measures from 1 ¼ to 2 inches in length and 1 to 1 3/8 inches wide. They have five toes. Toe # 1 rarely shows up in tracks. There are three palm pads, interdigital pads, and two additional pads, proximal pads, at the heel. The negative space between the pads has no fur. Hind tracks measure 1 ¼ to 3 ½ inches long and 7/8 to 1 ¾ inches in width. The fox squirrel stride walk measures between 4 and 6 inches and 3 ¾ to 4 ¼ inches wide. The bounding stride measures between 6 and 30 inches in length with a width of 4 to 7 inches (Elbroch, 2003).

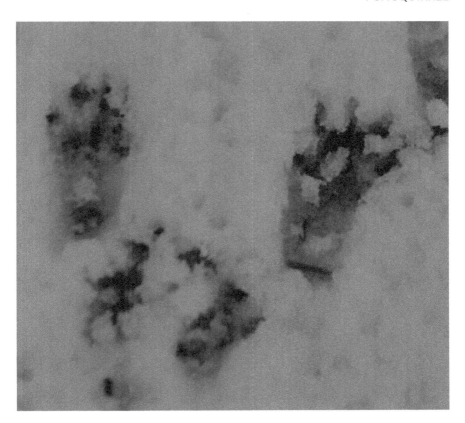

Personal Tracking Record:

Front Track ☐   Hind Track ☐   Scat ☐

Other Sign Found: _____
Date Found: _____
Habitat Found: _____
Place Found: _____
Parent's Initials: _____

Personal Tracking Record:

Front Track ☐   Hind Track ☐   Scat ☐

Other Sign Found: _____
Date Found: _____
Habitat Found: _____
Place Found: _____
Parent's Initials: _____

Personal Tracking Record:

Front Track ☐   Hind Track ☐   Scat ☐

Other Sign Found: _____
Date Found: _____
Habitat Found: _____
Place Found: _____
Parent's Initials: _____

 Cougar

Puma concolor

The cougar is the fourth largest of all the cats measuring 24 to 35 inches at the shoulder. Males can be 7 feet 9 inches long from nose to tail and weigh 115 to 220 pounds. Females can be 6 to 7 feet long from nose to tail and weigh from 64 to 141 pounds. Only tigers, lions and jaguars are larger. Cougars are not considered a large cat because technically, large cats (Panthera) can roar, while cougars cannot. They are often silent other than between mothers and her kittens. They are, however, well known for their screams to attract a mate during mating, which mimic a screaming woman. Their life expectancy is from 8 to 13 years.

Cougar Territory
IUCN Red List (2019)

The cougar's range is from the Canadian Yukon down to the Andes of South America. The cougar is very adaptable. It is found in most American habitat types. The cougar prefers a habitat with dense underbrush and rocky areas for stalking. It can live in open areas though. It uses topographic cover to assist it in remaining invisible. Cougars can run between 40 and 50 miles per hour. Cougars can leap 18 feet in one bound and 40 to 45 feet horizontally.

Cougars are ambush predators. They can take down bighorn sheep, moose, elk, deer, horses and cattle. They are opportunistic hunters. They will also prey on small mammals such as lizards, birds and fish. They will take one major prey every eight days. Once they have made a kill, the cougar will drag its prey to a cache spot and cover it with brush. They will then return later to continue to feed on their prey. The cougar is an obligate predator, meaning it survives exclusively on meat. A cougar can eat 20 pounds of meat in one sitting. This is in order to consume as much of its catch as possible due to the fresh kill smell, which alert other predators to the area.

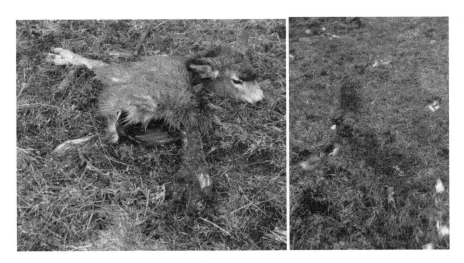

This is a typical cougar cache site. However, the cougar did not have enough dead foliage to cover his cache. On the right is the drag sign where the cougar dragged his prey in order to cache it.

The cougar is considered to be both nocturnal and crepuscular. Most cougars are solitary, never living in a pride or a pack. Only mothers live in groups with their kittens. Cougar mothers usually have litters between one and six cubs, but typically two. They are weaned at three months. They will go out hunting with the mother first to kill, sites then at 6 months will hunt on their own. The kittens are born with spots, but lose them by age 2 1/2 years old. They will leave their mother to establish their own territory around 2 years of age. Males will leave sooner. The kitten's survival rate is only one per litter.

Cougars can have dens to raise their kittens. They are great tree climbers. They are generally scared of large dogs and will climb trees for safety.

The cougar's front track is larger than the hind, it measuring between 2 ¾ to 3 7/8 inches in length and 2 7/8 to 4 7/8 inches in width. Four toes generally show up in the track. However, generally the track does not show claw marks. The palm of the pad, or interdigital pad, is fused to create one large pad. The leading edge of the pad has two lobes and the rear edge has three lobes. This interdigital pad forms a much larger portion of the track surface than the interdigital pads in canine tracks. The negative space, empty space, between the toes and interdigital pad forms a C shape. The front tracks are rounder than the hind tracks. The hind tracks measure 3 to 4 1/8 inches in length and 2 9/16 to 4 7/8 inches in width (Elbroch, 2003). The negative space forms a C or an H. The hind track is more elongated and symmetrically shaped than the front track.

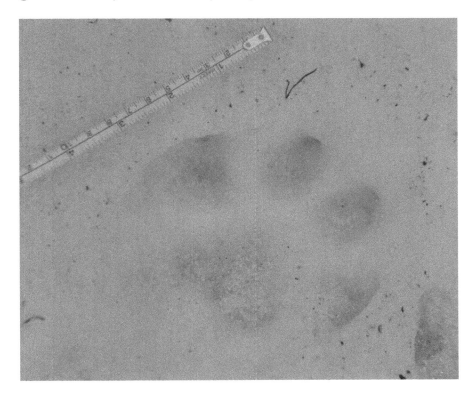

The cougar walking stride measures 15 to 28 inches in length and 4 to 11 inches in width. The cougar trot measures 29 to 38 inches in length and 3 to 5 ½ inches in width. The gallop measures 30 to 120 inches in length, and occasionally some bounds measure up to 25 feet (Elbroch, 2003).

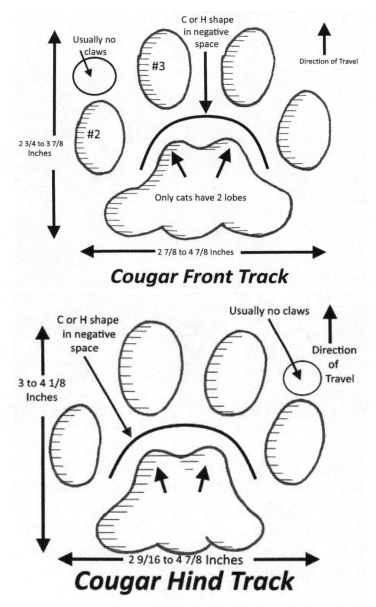

Cougar Front Track

Cougar Hind Track

Toe # 3 is slightly larger. Toe #1 does not show in the track. This demonstrates that this is a right track.

Cougar scat photographed one day after it rained on the scat

Personal Tracking Record:

Front Track ☐   Hind Track ☐   Scat ☐

Other Sign Found: _____
Date Found: _____
Habitat Found: _____
Place Found: _____
Parent's Initials: _____

Personal Tracking Record:

Front Track ☐   Hind Track ☐   Scat ☐

Other Sign Found: _____
Date Found: _____
Habitat Found: _____
Place Found: _____
Parent's Initials: _____

Personal Tracking Record:

Front Track ☐   Hind Track ☐   Scat ☐

Other Sign Found: _____
Date Found: _____
Habitat Found: _____
Place Found: _____
Parent's Initials: _____

 Bobcat

Lynx rufus

The bobcat has a gray to brown coat, black tufted ears, whiskers, black bars on its forelegs and a black-tipped stubby tail. The bobcat is usually smaller than the Canadian lynx, but, is about twice as a typical a domestic cat. The adult measures 18.7 inches to 49.2 inches long from head to tail and stands between 12 and 14 inches at the shoulder. Males weigh between 14 to 40 pounds while females weigh 8.8 to 33.7 pounds. Their hind legs are longer than their front. The more northern their habitat, the larger they tend to be. Bobcats tend to be **crepuscular**- meaning they are active during dawn and twilight, especially during the fall and winter. The bobcat will live between 7 and 10 years.

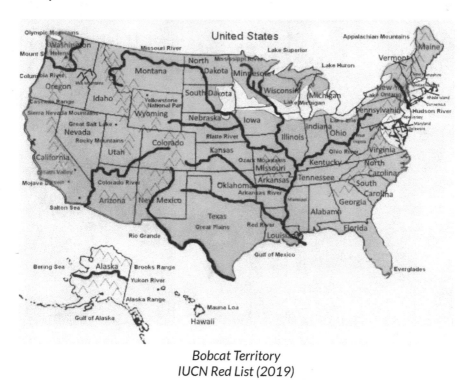

Bobcat Territory
IUCN Red List (2019)

All cats have large eyes with color vision and binocular vision enabling them to see as well as a human, but under declining light their sight is six times more accurate than a human's. Bobcats have sharp hearing as well, and are sensitive to high frequency sound. They rely on these senses for hunting prey rather than on their olfactory sense. Their range spans from Canada to southern Mexico. Their habitat is typically a rocky area or small cliff, rough ground, thickets, swamp, semi-desert and the edge of urban areas. Bobcats do not tolerate deep snow because they lack large padded feet that help walk on the snow. They will wait out heavy rain in sheltered areas. They are solitary and territorial. They mark their territory with claw marks, urine and feces. They tend to creep under brush very cautiously before approaching and stalking an animal.

Bobcats are able to survive a long time without food but will binge when food is abundant. They prey on larger animals they can kill and return to feed on them multiple times. Bobcats hunt by stalking their prey and can remain motionless for long periods of time, then ambushing it with a short sprint or pounce. They are an opportunistic predator that will vary what they feed on depending on what is available. The bobcat is much like the coyote in that their habitat is expanding and their numbers are increasing. The bobcat will hunt in areas with abundant prey by crouching or standing and waiting for its prey to wander close. For larger prey, the bobcat will stalk it from cover until they come within 20 to 35 feet before an attack charge. Bobcats are sprinters and will take 20 minutes to recover once they have made a charge. Like the cougar, the bobcat will make a cache site with its large kill by burying the carcass in snow or leaves. The bobcat prefers rabbits or hares but will hunt anything from insects, chickens, grouse and other birds, and small rodents to animals as large as deer.

During mating season, from winter to early spring, a dominant male will travel with a female and mate with her several times. They have a number of different courting behaviors including bumping, chasing and ambushing. The female will mate with multiple males and the male will mate with multiple females. If they don't have a home territory, they will not mate.

The front track of a bobcat measures 1 5/8 to 2 ½ inches in length and 1 3/8 to 2 5/8 inches in width. Four toes show up in the tracks. The interdigital pads of the track are fused, showing two lobes toward the toes and the heel has three lobes. The interdigital pad of the track takes up a large portion of the track. The negative space between the pads forms a C shape or an H shape. The nails do not normally show up in the track. The front track is larger and rounder than the hind track. The hind track measures 1 9/16 inches to 2 ½ inches in length and 1 3/16 to 2 5/8 inches wide. The bobcat walking stride measures 6 to 14 inches in length and 5 to 9 ½ inches wide. The gallop stride measures 16 to 48 inches in length (Elbroch, 2003).

The largest difference between the bobcat and the lynx is the size of their paws. Lynx have huge paws compared to their body size. The bobcat has a black short tail with black stripes, black at the tip and white on the bottom. Their coats are shorter than the lynx with more spots. Lynx are more specialized in hunting the snowshoe hare while the bobcat is an opportunistic predator.

Because toe #3 is slightly larger, this shows this photo is a right track.

Usually you don't see claws; they will be there if the cat is trying to get traction.

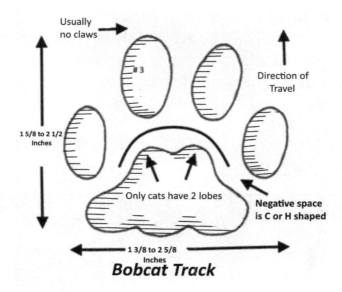

Usually no claws →

3

↑ Direction of Travel

1 5/8 to 2 1/2 Inches

Only cats have 2 lobes

Negative space is C or H shaped

← 1 3/8 to 2 5/8 Inches →

Bobcat Track

Toe # 3 is slightly larger. Toe #1 does not show, which demonstrates this drawing is a right foot track.

Bobcat scat: he had difficulty with scratching and covering

Personal Tracking Record:

Front Track ☐   Hind Track ☐   Scat ☐

Other Sign Found: _____
Date Found: _____
Habitat Found: _____
Place Found: _____
Parent's Initials: _____

Personal Tracking Record:

Front Track ☐   Hind Track ☐   Scat ☐

Other Sign Found: _____
Date Found: _____
Habitat Found: _____
Place Found: _____
Parent's Initials: _____

Personal Tracking Record:

Front Track ☐   Hind Track ☐   Scat ☐

Other Sign Found: _____
Date Found: _____
Habitat Found: _____
Place Found: _____
Parent's Initials: _____

 # American Alligator

Alligator mississippiensis

The American alligator is dark gray or black in color compared to the American crocodile which is green in color. It has a U-shaped snout while the crocodile has a V-shaped snout. The alligator's top teeth show when its mouth is closed, making it look like it is smiling. In comparison, the American crocodile's top and bottom teeth both show when its mouth is closed making it look mean.

An American Aligator's teeth fall out continuously. One Aligator can have more than 3000 teeth in one lifetime.

The alligator's legs are more beneath it when it walks while the crocodile's legs are a bit more out to the sides making the footprints spread further apart.

The American alligator grows one foot a year for the first six years. One they reach six feet long, they are considered adults. Adult males average between 11 to 15 feet in length and can weigh up to 1,000 pounds. Adult females measure 8 1/2 feet up to almost 10 feet.

Alligators are predators that primarily hunt at night and will eat any animal they can fit in their mouths.

Did you know? American alligators will eat anything they can fit into their mouths, including other alligators!! This is known as cannibalism.

The juveniles will start with insects, shrimp, and small fish. The adults eat fish, amphibians, reptiles, birds, mammals, and other alligators. If they capture a large prey, the alligator will drag it under water, drown it then eat. They have a special adaptation called a **gular fold.** This allows them to capture prey while completely submerged under water without allowing water into their lungs.

American Alligator Territory
IUCN Red List (2019)

The American alligator lives in fresh water from North Carolina south to Florida and west to eastern Texas. Cypress swamps, marshes, rivers and lakes are preferred. They can also be found in canals and any body of fresh water including ponds on golf courses. The American alligator is considered a keystone species.

They dig out alligator holes, usually in swamps, looking like a small pond. This is a hole that retains water even during the dry season. These alligator holes create a habitat for other animals including fish, turtles, snakes and birds that would otherwise not survive the dry season. These small ponds are one sign that alligators are in the area.

Did you know? North American Alligators have a strong homing instinct. Scientists have discovered that when problematic alligators have been moved to a new home, they can find their way home even after being moved 100 miles!!

Alligators are **ectotherms**, cold blooded, cannot regulate their own body temperatures but match the temperature of their surroundings. They warm themselves by sunning out of the water on banks. On hot days they can be seen on the banks with their mouths open. This allows them to cool down. They are most active when the temperature is between 82 and 92 degrees. The alligator will stop feeding when the temperatures drop below 70 degrees Fahrenheit. Alligators construct a burrow next to an alligator hole or near open water. When the temperature drops below 55 degrees, they will burrow and become dormant for the winter.

Crocodile is on the left, the alligator is on the right.

Three-year-old juvenile American alligator.

Do not try this at home; he was under the supervision of professionals!

If an alligator survives to adulthood, it can live up to 35 years old in the wild. A mother alligator can lay 32 to 46 white hard-shelled eggs. Female alligators will build a mound of soil, mud, vegetation, or debris for her nest. The mound is 3 ½ to 6 feet across and 1 to 2 feet high. This mound is usually found in an area cleared of vegetation by the mother from 13 to 18 feet across. She lays 3 to 3 ½ inch long cylindrical eggs that are about 1 ½ inches in diameter and buries them 3 to 14 inches deep. She is protective of her nest and hatchlings because they are prey for other animals. The temperature of the nest can determine the sex of the hatchlings. If the temperature ranges between 82 and 86 degrees the hatchlings will be female. If the temperature ranges between 90 and 93 degrees the hatchlings will be male. If the nest is between 86 and 90 degrees the hatchlings will be both male and female. On average only 4 hatchlings will live to be adults because of the number of other animals that eat them.

The mother alligator will defend the nest against predators throughout the 65 day incubation period. When the eggs are ready to hatch, the young will begin to make a high-pitched noise from inside their eggs calling for their mother. The mother will then dig down to the eggs and help open any eggs that have not hatched. She will then carry her young to the water. Mother alligators have been known to defend their young for more than a year.

Adult American alligator tracks (notice the tail drag marks)

The American alligator's prints show five toes for the front foot and four toes for the hind foot. The hind footprint size correlates to the size of the alligator body length. The body length is 14 times that of the size of the hind foot.

Alligators have 5 toes on their front feet and 4 toes on their hind feet.

Alligator Front Track

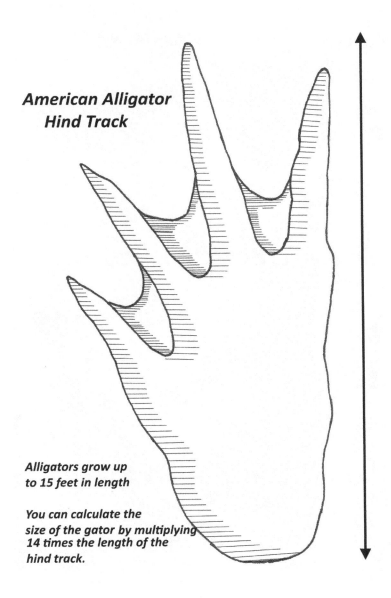

American Alligator
Hind Track

Alligators grow up
to 15 feet in length

You can calculate the
size of the gator by multiplying
14 times the length of the
hind track.

Personal Tracking Record:

Front Track ☐   Hind Track ☐   Scat ☐

Other Sign Found: _____

Date Found: _____

Habitat Found: _____

Place Found: _____

Parent's Initials: _____

Personal Tracking Record:

Front Track ☐   Hind Track ☐   Scat ☐

Other Sign Found: _____

Date Found: _____

Habitat Found: _____

Place Found: _____

Parent's Initials: _____

Personal Tracking Record:

Front Track ☐   Hind Track ☐   Scat ☐

Other Sign Found: _____

Date Found: _____

Habitat Found: _____

Place Found: _____

Parent's Initials: _____

 # Green Sea Turtle

Chelonia mydas

The green sea turtle, C. mydas, has a flattened body where its teardrop-shaped upper shell- **carapace**, is more flattened as is its under shell the **plastron.**

It has a beaked head with a short neck and long flippers instead of arms or legs. Adult green sea turtles have one claw on each flipper. Adults grow to five feet long and weigh between 150 and 420 pounds. Its beak lacks a hook and it cannot pull its neck into its shell. The green sea turtle's carapace has five central **scutes** with four pairs of scutes on each side. The shell color patterns change over time. The hatchlings have an upper shell that is mostly black with light-colored plastrons. The juvenile's carapace turn dark brown to olive colored. Adult carapaces are either completely brown, spotted or mottled brown. They gets their name from the green fat found beneath their shell.

Green Sea Turtle Territory
IUCN Red List (2019)

The green sea turtle lives in different habitats depending on its age. They lay eggs on sandy beaches. Adult turtles spend most of their time in shallow coastal waters including coral reefs, salt marshes, and close-to-shore seagrass beds. They live primarily in the water and are considered **aquatic** species. They are found around the world in warm tropical to subtropical waters where temperatures are greater than 45 degrees Fahrenheit.

The green sea turtles live in convergence zones in the bare open oceans for the first five years of life. **Convergence zones** are areas where two different surface waters come together, usually mixing two different temperatures or salinities of water (degree of saltiness). They swim in deep **pelagic** waters -upper layers of the open ocean. Hatchlings are carnivorous eating pelagic organisms, fish eggs, mollusks, jellyfish, small invertebrates, worms, sponges, algae, and crustaceans. Adult sea turtles are strictly herbivores eating seagrasses.

Green sea turtles can migrate long distances between feeding sites and nesting sites. Adult females often return to the exact beach from which they hatched. Females mate every two to four years. Males visit the beaches where they hatched every year attempting to reproduce. **Natal homing** is the ability to return to their hatching beach.

After mating in the water, the female travels up the beach above the high tide, line where she digs a hole with her hind flippers. These holes range between 11 and 22 inches deep. She deposits between 85 and 200 eggs and then covers it again with sand. The size of the clutch depends on the age of the female. The female will then return to the sea to mate again. She can lay eggs three to five times in one mating season.

The temperature of the nest determines the sex of the turtles. They will hatch between 50 and 70 days. The eggs hatch at night and the entire clutch will emerge together and instinctively head into the water. Due to all of the predators, only 1% of the hatchlings become adults. Adult sea turtles can live up to 80 years.

Uses both flippers at the same time to push itself forward.

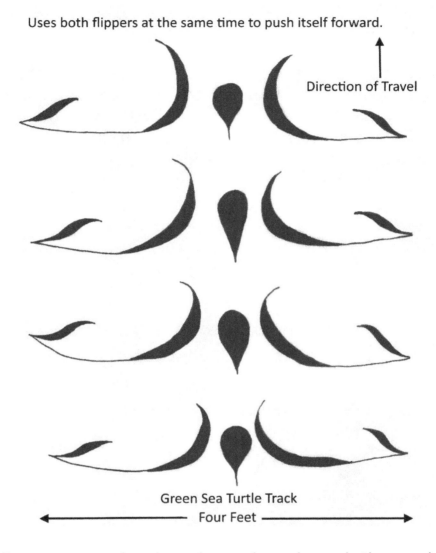

Direction of Travel

Green Sea Turtle Track
← Four Feet →

Green sea turtles drag themselves through the sand by pulling with both flippers at the same time. The straight flipper marks line up in pairs. In the center of the trail, you will usually see a line left by a tail, including marks left by the tip of the tail.

The green sea turtle, Chelonia mydas, is considered endangered by the IUCN Red List.

Green sea turtles breathe air, but spend most of their lives under water. Although they surface for breaths of air, they can sleep under water for several hours. The more active they are, the more frequently they have to surface for air. Evading predators and eating require higher oxygen demands.

Did you know? Green sea turtles can live up to 80 years old? Scientists believe that they are not mature enough to mate until they are between 30 and 50 years old!!

Personal Tracking Record:

Front Track ☐   Hind Track ☐   Scat ☐

Other Sign Found: _____

Date Found: _____

Habitat Found: _____

Place Found: _____

Parent's Initials: _____

Personal Tracking Record:

Front Track ☐   Hind Track ☐   Scat ☐

Other Sign Found: _____

Date Found: _____

Habitat Found: _____

Place Found: _____

Parent's Initials: _____

Personal Tracking Record:

Front Track ☐   Hind Track ☐   Scat ☐

Other Sign Found: _____

Date Found: _____

Habitat Found: _____

Place Found: _____

Parent's Initials: _____

 American Bullfrog

Lithobates catesbeianus

The American bullfrog is an olive green with or without bands of grayish brown. The bullfrog's belly is off-white blotched with yellow or gray. The eyes are prominent with brown irises and almond-shaped pupils. The eardrums are seen just behind the eyes. The size of the eardrum identifies the sex. If the eardrum, **tympana,** is larger than the eye it is a male. If the eardrum is the same size as the eye it is a female. The front legs are short and the hind legs are long. The front toes are not webbed while the back toes have webbing, with the exception of the unwebbed fourth toe. The males are generally larger than the females and have yellow throats. Bullfrogs measure from about 3.6 to 6 inches from nose to bottom. Adults can weigh up to 1.1 pounds. The American bullfrog is **ectothermic.** Ectotherms cannot regulate their body temperature and their body temperature depends on external sources like sunlight.

The American bullfrog habitat is permanent bodies of water, including lakes and ponds. They are usually found near the water's edge. They are found in every state in the United States except Hawaii and Alaska.

American Bullfrog
IUCN Red List (2019)

Female American bullfrogs can lay one or two clutches per season with about 12,000 to 20,000 eggs. These eggs are laid in a film or froth on the surface of the water in an area that has some vegetation protection. After the eggs are laid, there is no parental involvement. The tadpoles hatch after about 4 to 5 days when the eggs have been laid.

Tadpole

Tadpoles graze primarily on aquatic plants. They are independent right away and able to forage for themselves. Only 18 % of the tadpoles make it to maturity due to predators.

Tadpoles have gills and a tail. This tail eventually is adsorbed as the tadpole grows legs and turns into a froglet.

Tadpole metamorphosis
(Check out his legs)
Look Mom, no hands!

Froglet

The **metamorphosis**- a change in form from one thing into a completely different form in nature, takes about one year. In mountain habitats it can take 2 years. An American bullfrog does not become sexually mature for one year after it has completed its metamorphosis.

Bullfrogs are opportunistic ambush predators that prey on any small animal they can overpower and fit in their mouths. Bullfrogs have eaten rodents, small reptiles, amphibians, birds, crayfish, insects and even bats. They have the amazing ability to adjust for light refraction at the water surface by striking at a position behind the target's perceived location. The movement of the prey triggers the feeding behavior. First, the frog performs a single body rotation ending with the frog aimed toward the prey; second, the frog leaps if necessary. Once within striking distance, the bullfrog takes a ballistic lunge that ends with the mouth opening while its eyes are closed. At this same time its mucus coated tongue strikes toward its prey, often engulfing it while its jaws continue to travel forward to close just as their tongue is retracted. Large prey that do not fit are often stuffed in with their hands.

Bullfrogs are able to jump distances 10 times their body length.

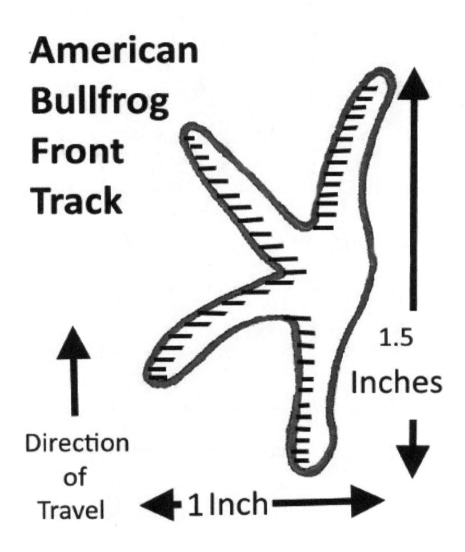

American Bullfrog Front Track

Direction of Travel

1.5 Inches

1 Inch

American Bullfrog Hind Track

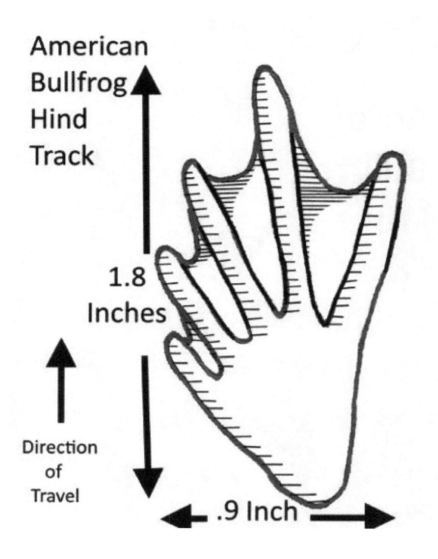

1.8 Inches

Direction of Travel

.9 Inch

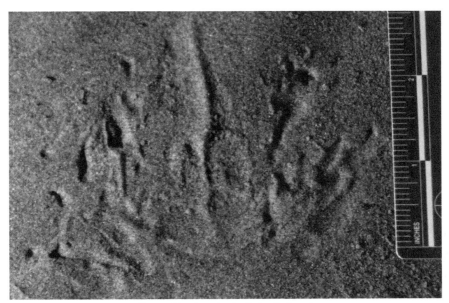

Front, hind and whole body track

How to Catch a Bullfrog

Prepare your tools. Bullfrogs can be caught bare-handed, but your hands should be clean and wet. Bullfrogs absorb things through their skin, so dirty hands could harm the frog. A fishing net with a long handle works well. You'll also need a bright flashlight and a large plastic bucket with a lid if your are going to be transporting the frogs.

Find a good bullfrog habitat. Bullfrogs live in fresh-water lakes, ponds, rivers and streams. They tend to live where there is shade, like trees, cattails, with very minimal to no current.

Check the bullfrog season and make sure you are hunting on public land.

Never hunt for bullfrogs in a conservation area.

Make sure you have permission to hunt on private property.

Listen for the bullfrog calls. Bullfrogs make a low-tones bass-like call that sounds like a low "Ruuuuumm Ruuuuuumm". Between early spring and summer, the male bullfrogs will sing together in a deep, roaring tone. This is an indicator where you can find them.

Go hunting at night with your parent's permission. It is easier to see the bullfrogs at night, so it is recommended that you wait until it's fairly dark.

Shine a bright flashlight along the shoreline to find the frogs. Move the beam of light slowly along the shoreline until you see a pair of bullfrog eyes. If its eyes are wide apart, it is a big bullfrog.

Move slowly and quietly. You want to be very conscious of the amount of noise that you make so you don't scare the frogs.

"Jack the bullfrog" by shining the light in their eyes. The bullfrog will freeze. Take this opportunity to catch the bullfrog with your hands or your net.

Move quickly and use a firm grip. Bullfrogs are quick to respond to movement, so you'll need to pounce quickly and use a firm grip around its upper thighs with legs together. This minimizes their chance of escape.

Place the frog in a closed container. If you don't close the container, they will escape.

Once you've had a chance to study your bullfrog, release it to live free and in the wild.

Did you know?
Bullfrogs will eat anything they can fit in their mouths, including mice, bats, and other frogs. This is known as cannibalism. They will use their hands to help shove it into their mouths if it is a tight fit.

Personal Tracking Record:
Front Track ☐   Hind Track ☐   Scat ☐

Other Sign Found: _____
Date Found: _____
Habitat Found: _____
Place Found: _____
Parent's Initials: _____

Personal Tracking Record:
Front Track ☐   Hind Track ☐   Scat ☐

Other Sign Found: _____
Date Found: _____
Habitat Found: _____
Place Found: _____
Parent's Initials: _____

Personal Tracking Record:
Front Track ☐   Hind Track ☐   Scat ☐

Other Sign Found: _____
Date Found: _____
Habitat Found: _____
Place Found: _____
Parent's Initials: _____

 Western Toad

Anaxyrus boreas

The western toad, Anaxyrus boreas, is a large toad measuring between 2.2 and 5.1 inches long from nose tip to bottom. It is gray in color or greenish with a cream-colored stripe going down its back. It has parotoid glands that are widely separated and larger than their upper eyelids and that secrete a mild poison. It has horizonal pupils instead of diagonal pupils but does not have cranial crests. On the bottom of its back feet it has two brown tubercles. These tubercles can make a mark in their tracks. These tubercles do not have sharp edges. Uniquely, the males make a repeated chirping sound due to the lack of a vocal sac.

Western Toad Territory
IUCN Red List (2019)

Western toads are spread throughout the mountains of northwestern North America, ranging from sea level to elevations near the treeline. They occupy desert streams, grasslands and mountain meadows; additionally, they are commonly found in heavily wooded regions. They are usually found near ponds or lakes, streams, and rivers.

Western toads are active from January to October, depending on the latitude and elevation and hibernate over the winter. Adult Western toads will dig burrows in soft ground or take over the burrow of a small mammals to hibernate. These burrows are chosen so they do not freeze over the winter. Western toads are more active at night at lower elevations and in northern areas of their range; at higher elevations they are more diurnal. They remain fairly close to water during the daytime but may travel widely at night.

Western toads are **terrestrial**, found more on solid ground. They are **ectotherms**, they rely on the environment to control their body temperatures by basking and evaporative cooling. In order to avoid loosing too much moisture, they usually spend the daytime hours on the forest floor in the soil under rocks, logs, and stumps or in rodent burrows.

Western toads wait for their prey on the surface of the ground or in shallow burrows. They primarily eat bees, beetles, ants and spiders. They may also eat sow-bugs, grasshoppers, crayfish, and flies.

In Oregon the breeding age for male western toads is three years and between four and five years for females. Male toads tend to breed every year, but females breed at less regular intervals. Male Western Toads will develop a dark patch on their thumbs when they are ready for breeding. Male toads are found more in wet habitats and females are found in larger number in drier habitats. Female Western Toads will lay their eggs in shallow ponds, pools or slow moving water preferably with some protective vegetation. The eggs are black and 1.5 to 1.8 millimeters in diameter and are laid in long wide strings of double layered jelly in two rows. This is specifically a Western Toad egg pattern and can differentiate from other toads due to this pattern.

These eggs hatch over the next ten days. These tadpoles have horizontal pupils rather than diagonal. These tad poles are black or dark brown, their eyes are midway between the dorsal midline and the edge of the head. It takes 2 months for these tadpoles to complete metamorphosis into a toad.

Western Toad Front Track

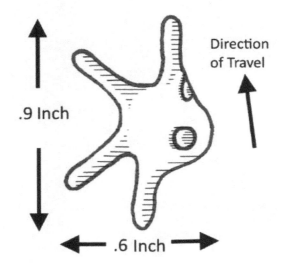

.9 Inch

.6 Inch

Direction
of Travel

Western Toad Hind Track

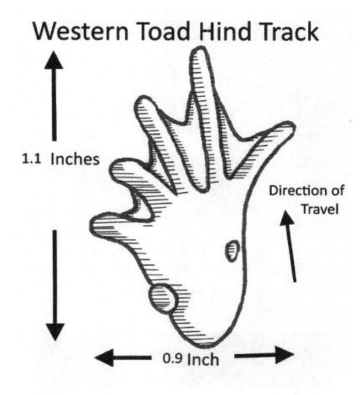

1.1 Inches

Direction of Travel

0.9 Inch

The western toad tends to walk rather than jump like a frogs. Because they are slower movers, they are more vulnerable to predators. The western toad defends itself by producing skin toxins that most predators avoid.

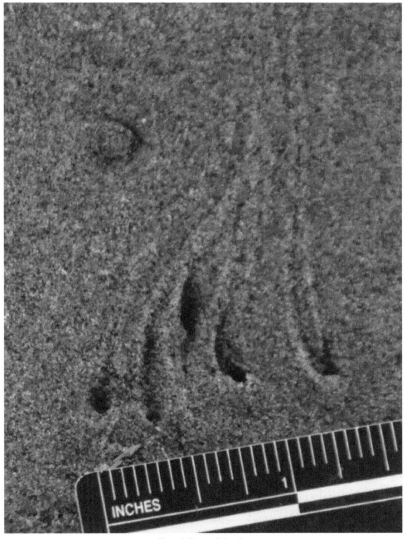

Toad Drag Marks

Personal Tracking Record:

Front Track ☐   Hind Track ☐   Scat ☐

Other Sign Found: _____
Date Found: _____
Habitat Found: _____
Place Found: _____
Parent's Initials: _____

Personal Tracking Record:

Front Track ☐   Hind Track ☐   Scat ☐

Other Sign Found: _____
Date Found: _____
Habitat Found: _____
Place Found: _____
Parent's Initials: _____

Personal Tracking Record:

Front Track ☐   Hind Track ☐   Scat ☐

Other Sign Found: _____
Date Found: _____
Habitat Found: _____
Place Found: _____
Parent's Initials: _____

 Prairie Rattlesnake

Crotalus viridis

Photo courtesy of Troy LaFleur

Prairie rattlesnakes are found in forests, brush, caves, close to streams, and rocky areas, but primarily in grasslands and prairies. They will take over prairie dog dens when they have been vacated. They are more likely to be found on south-facing slopes with rocky outcrops. They will migrate up to 7 miles from their den for hunting. In the winter they brumate. **Brumation** is similar to hibernation among mammals. During brumation, a rattlesnake will be sluggish and sometimes not moving at all for the entire winter. Generally, rattlesnakes will find hibernaculums that are somewhat insulated within their environment. A **hibernaculum** is the place where the snake spends these cold times of inclement weather usually below the frost line, deep enough where the ground does not freeze. At times they congregate in the same hibernaculum by the hundreds. During hot weather they are nocturnal but during the cooler months they are active during the daytime.

Prairie Rattlesnake Territory
IUCN Red List (2019)

Prairie rattlesnakes are **ectotherms,** considered cold blooded or having to rely on the temperature of their surrounding for their body temperature. They rely more on the temperature of the ground for their body heat than the temperature of the air. They are able to move more quickly when their body temperature is higher.

Prairie rattlesnakes have narrow necks and a triangle-shaped head. They can grow to more than three feet in length. The maximum recorded size was close to five feet. Prairie rattlesnakes vary in color. Most are greenish gray, olive green, or greenish brown, but some are yellowish or light brown. They are covered with brown or black blotches which turn into rings on the tail. Females usually have fewer rings than males. Their underbelly is cream to white colored. These blotches have a darker brown ring around them and is separated by a trace of white. They have between 33 to 55 distinctive blotches.

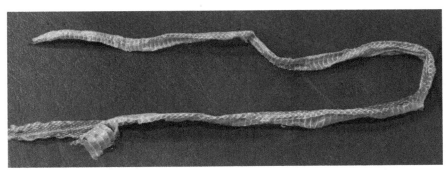

*Kids, you too can freak out your mother with a shed snakeskin.
I know I was!!*

Prairie rattlesnakes have a venom with neurotoxic, which stop the nerves from firing and kills the prey by stopping their breathing and hemotoxic properties which kills its prey but also destroys tissue which helps with their digestion. When they bite they can inject 20% to 55% of their venom supply in a single bite. They can be lethal to humans. They have a pair of hollow fangs to deliver this venom. These fangs are long and curved folding against the roof of their mouth when not in use. They are able to point these fangs forward when they strike. If they break a fang a new fang will grow in to replace it. Their fangs and teeth are replaced regularly. The amount of venom injected is controlled by muscles that surround the venom glands.

The prairie rattlesnake has a wide variety of diet, including prairie dogs, voles, shrews, ground squirrels, small rabbits, rats or mice, some birds, and even other snakes. This is due to their extensive habitat range.

The prairie rattle snake gives birth to live young. Their mating season occurs between March and May. Females only breed every 2 to 3 years and give birth to 4 to 25 live snakes in August to September. It is common for the to give birth in communal dens. The hatchlings are born about 22 to 28 cm long and are as venomous as adults. They do not have rattles at this time.

Because of their small size, the survival rate for these newborns is limited. They are prey for birds such as hawks, eagles, and short eared-owls and for king-snakes. The prairie rattle-snake reaches sexual maturity after 3 years.

The species of snake cannot be determined by its tracks. There are five primary types of snake locomotion: lateral undulations, concertina, side-winding, slide pushing, and rectilinear. Most snake species will use one to two forms of locomotion. The snake's body size and shape influences the tracks. In addition, the temperature of the ground and air influences the snake tracks, as does the terrain, including the soil type, and amount of plants, rocks, slope, and cover.

Lateral undulation is the most familiar snake movement, creating classic snake tracks. Waves of muscular motion travel down the length of the snake's body toward its tail. As the snake comes in contact with an object like a stick, the part of the body nearest the object exerts force against that object, and deforms locally around it. When the snake pushes against various objects, overall it will move forward. (Tkaczyk, 2015)

Lateral Undulations

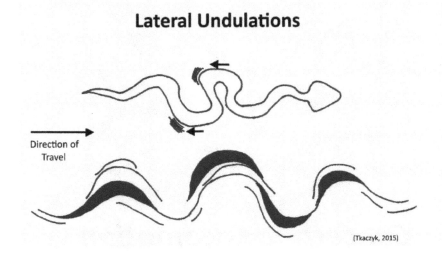

Direction of Travel

(Tkaczyk, 2015)

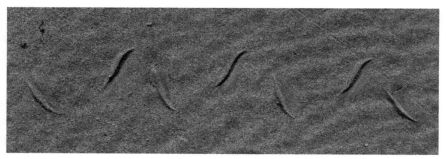

Lateral undulations
Photo courtesy of Filip Tkaczyk

Concertina locomotion movement leaves a totally different set of tracks. Here the snake pulls its up the body into bends and then straightening out the bends. This form of locomotion is most common in small spaces or when climbing. These kinds of tracks are rarely seen as they generally require sub straight to present in narrow spaces. (Tkaczyk, 2015)

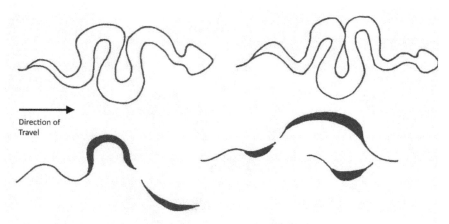

Direction of Travel

Concertina Locomotion

(Tkaczyk, 2015)

Slide pushing results in unusually wide, broad tracks. The snake forcefully pushes its body in very large undulations that slide sideways and move it widely across the surface. This track is generally found when the snake is frightened or disturbed on a smooth surface and it has attempted to escape. The snake's body uses enough force while pushing down to move its body forward in small movements. Usually the rear half or two thirds of its body create this motion. (Tkaczyk, 2015)

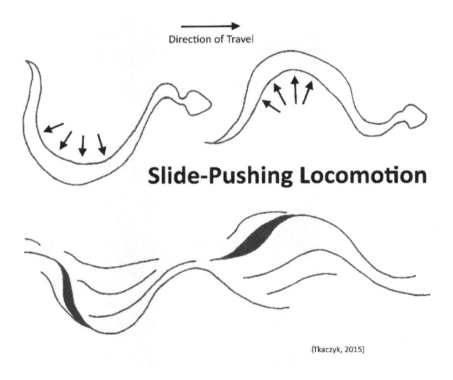

Direction of Travel

Slide-Pushing Locomotion

(Tkaczyk, 2015)

Side-winding is used by many snakes when traveling over smooth, slippery or unstable surfaces. The snake sends a wave down its body so that it rolls from head to tail and the wave portion is off the ground as the body moves. The track length is representative of the length of the snake. This track is more commonly found in sandy areas. (Tkaczyk, 2015)

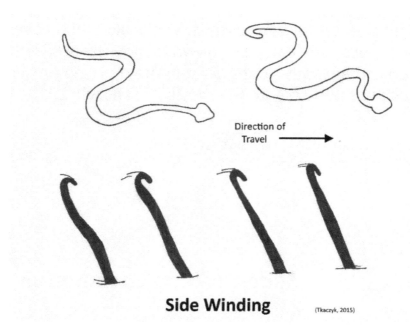

Direction of Travel ⟶

Side Winding (Tkaczyk, 2015)

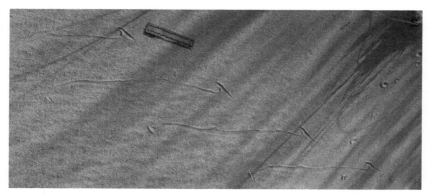

Side Winding tracks
Photo courtesy of Filip Tkaczyk

Rectilinear locomotion leaves tracks that are pretty much in a straight line. This is used primarily by larger and heavier snakes. It is found in areas of open ground. It moves by first lifting the belly scales slightly from the ground, then pulling them forward and then downward and backward. This movement is similar to the movement of a caterpillar. (Tkaczyk, 2015)

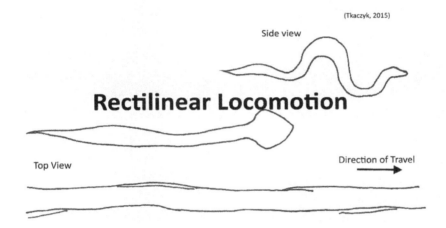

(Tkaczyk, 2015)

Side view

Rectilinear Locomotion

Top View

Direction of Travel

Personal Tracking Record:
Front Track ☐   Hind Track ☐   Scat ☐

Other Sign Found: _____
Date Found: _____
Habitat Found: _____
Place Found: _____
Parent's Initials: _____

Personal Tracking Record:
Front Track ☐   Hind Track ☐   Scat ☐

Other Sign Found: _____
Date Found: _____
Habitat Found: _____
Place Found: _____
Parent's Initials: _____

Personal Tracking Record:
Front Track ☐   Hind Track ☐   Scat ☐

Other Sign Found: _____
Date Found: _____
Habitat Found: _____
Place Found: _____
Parent's Initials: _____

 Wild Turkey

Meleagris gallopavo

Wild turkeys can fly! They sleep in trees, which is called **roosting**. They come down and mainly walk to feed, mate, and nest but return to the trees again to sleep. Adults have long reddish yellow to grayish green legs. Their bodies and feathers are blackish and dark brown with a bronze green iridescent sheen that is more complex in males. Adult males have featherless heads, a red long neck, and red wattles on their throats and necks. Adult males are called **toms** or gobblers, while juvenile males are called **jakes**. The difference between the tom and the jake is that a jake has a shorter beard and his tail, when fanned has longer feathers in the middle. When males get excited, the fleshy flap on top of their bill, the wattle, will expand and the bare skin on their head and neck all become red and engorged with blood. Toms will spread their tails in a fan and fluff their feathers to gain a hen's attention. These tail feathers have a white or rust color tip on the end. Males are much larger than females, which are known as hens. Males have a long tuft of hair, called a beard, growing from the center of the breast called a beard.

Females have feathers that are much duller overall than the males and are shades of brown and gray. Their heads will look more gray or white. Turkeys mate in the spring. During the mating season they will stay in small groups of three or four males or three to four females. An older hen will stay on the perimeter of the group as a sentry and send a warning call if there is danger, while the males will perform their mating dance and court the females. Turkeys are **polygamous,** mating with as many hens as they can. They will put on a display for the hens by puffing out their feathers and spreading their tail feathers in a fan while strutting. The color of their head will change with their mood. They use gobbling, drumming, booming and spitting as signs of dominance. These courtships begin during March and April many times while they are still flocked together in the winter area.

When mating is finished, females will search for a nest area. Their nests are shallow, dirt depressions with woody vegetation. Hens will lay 10 to 14 eggs, usually one per day, and incubate for 28 days. Occasionally, hens will **nest parasitize,** laying eggs in another hen's nest. Only the hen will incubate the eggs. Incubation lasts between 25 and 31 days.

The turkey chicks are called **poults**. The poults leave the nest soon after hatching. The hens will tend the poults and **brood**, sit on them, at night for several weeks. The poults will feed themselves. The poults can make short flights at 1 to 2 weeks of age, but are not fully grown for several months.

Turkeys are omnivores. They forage on the ground eating grasses, and will also forage in shrubs and small trees. They prefer nuts, seeds, berries, roots, insects, and worms. On occasion, they will eat small lizards and snakes. They generally feed in the early morning and in the late afternoon.

The wild turkey's habitat is hardwood and mixed conifer forest with nearby pastures, orchards, seasonal marshes, and a body of water or streams and rivers. Turkeys prefer a mature forest with a variety of tree species. They fly beneath the canopy of trees to find perches. Turkeys will usually fly close to the ground for more than a quarter of mile.

Wild Turkey Territory
IUCN Red List (2019)

Turkey tracks measure between 3 ¾ and 5 inches in length and 4 to 5 ¼ inches wide (Elbroch, 2001). Toe # 1 can show up in the tracks but not always.

Walking stride measures between 5 and 13 inches with a run stride up to 33 inches. Because much of the year they are a flock species, look for multiple bird tracks.

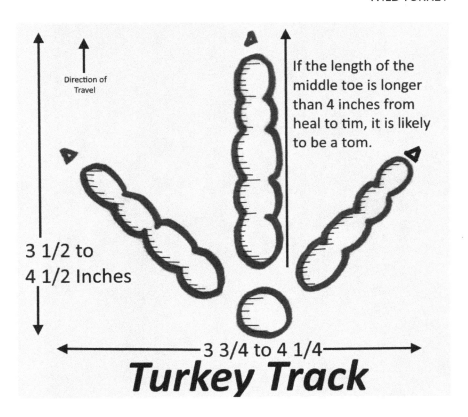

Direction of Travel

If the length of the middle toe is longer than 4 inches from heal to tim, it is likely to be a tom.

3 1/2 to 4 1/2 Inches

3 3/4 to 4 1/4

Turkey Track

Turkeys have three toes, and the toes of a tom are longer than those of a hen. A track that measures more than 4 inches from the heel to the tip of the middle toe is more likely to be a tom. Also, any tracks that show the segmentation clearly between the joints are from a heavy turkey, which is likely to be a tom.

Turkey scat can even distinguish between a hen and a tom. Droppings from a tom are elongated and measure about 2 inches, with a bulb on one end or a J hook. Droppings from a hen tend to be more globular and spiral or popcorn shaped.

The turkey nest is found on dry ground, usually near the strutting ground of the male. The nest is found in a depression in dry leaves, often under a log or brush or at the base of a tree. The lining is almost entirely made of leaves. They can have between 8 and 15 eggs. The average egg size is 63 x 45 mm. They are short oval to long oval, sometimes quite pointed. The shell is smooth with little or no gloss. They are pale buff or buffy white in color, evenly marked with reddish brown or pinkish buff spots or dots.

Personal Tracking Record:
Front Track ☐　　Hind Track ☐　　Scat ☐

Other Sign Found: _____
Date Found: _____
Habitat Found: _____
Place Found: _____
Parent's Initials: _____

Personal Tracking Record:
Front Track ☐　　Hind Track ☐　　Scat ☐

Other Sign Found: _____
Date Found: _____
Habitat Found: _____
Place Found: _____
Parent's Initials: _____

Personal Tracking Record:
Front Track ☐　　Hind Track ☐　　Scat ☐

Other Sign Found: _____
Date Found: _____
Habitat Found: _____
Place Found: _____
Parent's Initials: _____

 Ring-necked Pheasant

Phasianus colchicus

The ring-necked pheasant weighs between 1.1 and 6.6 pounds. Males measure between 24 and 35 inches. Males are barred bright gold and brown in color with green, purple and white markings. The small head is green with a small brown crest and a distinctive red wattle. They have a long iridescent green neck with a white ring. The males' very long tail is copper in color with thin black bars. They have plump bodies with long pointed tails. Hens are a duller multi brown color all over, they have paler scaling on their underparts and black spotting on the sides and tails. Hens measure between 20 to 25 inches. Juveniles appear similar to hens with a shorter tail until the males mature and begin to grown their bright colors.

The ring-necked pheasant's native habitat is a grass-land near water with small copses of trees. They are also found in woodlands, farmlands, scrub, and wetlands.

Ring-necked Pheasant Territory
IUCN Red List (2019)

They are very social birds. They will form loose flocks even outside of the breeding season with a small group of males but a larger flock of females. They are very timid around humans and will retreat to safety. The pheasant is able to fly a short distance to evade predators but they prefer to run. When they fly, their cruising flight speed is between 27 and 38 miles per hour. When evading predators, they can fly up to 56 miles per hour. They feed on the ground but will roost in trees. Ring-necked pheasant will forage on the ground in fields eating waste grain, other seeds and insects, however, will sometimes feed in trees. They feed on fruit, seeds, leaves, and a wide range of invertebrates. They also eat some small snakes, lizards, small mammals and rarely some birds. Ring-necked pheasants will generally feed on the ground, however, will sometimes feed in trees. They can be seen scratching with their feet or digging with their beak for food.

Pheasant hens are mottled brown so that they are camouflaged while incubating their egg Their nests are on the ground and more vulnerable to predators.

Males will breed with multiple hens and are often found near a harem of hens that flock in his territory. The male will defend their territory by perching on a raised perch, crowing loudly while drumming their wings. Males will court their hen by strutting in a half circle around the female tilting their tail and back towards her. His face wattle is swollen and he droops the wing closest to the hen.

Pheasants nest on the ground in dense cover. The ring-necked pheasant build their nest in bushy pastures, open fields, and hayfields. The nest is found in a natural hollow or in a shallow depression scraped out by the hen. It is lined with forbes, grasses, leaves, weeds and feathers. It is usually concealed by surrounding vegetation. They nest on the ground and will produce a clutch of about 10 eggs. Occasionally hens will **parasitize** other Ring-necked pheasant's nests by laying eggs in another hen's nest or even other birds. Clutches of more than 18 eggs are likely to be the result of two hens. The eggs are oval with a smooth shell that has a slight gloss. They are a rich brownish olive color or olive buff color. They average 41mm x 33 mm in size. They lay between 6 and 15 eggs. Incubation is for 23 to 28 days by the female only. The downy chicks leave the nest shortly after hatching and are capable of flight in about 12 days.

The ring-necked pheasant track measures between 2 and 2 15/16 inches in length and measures 2 and 2 ¾ inches in width. Toe # 1 tends to show up well in the tracks; this is the toe that is off the back of their heel. The walk/run stride measures between 2 ½ and 9 inches with a running stride up to 24 inches between tracks (Elbroch, 2001). Tracks may be seen in the open because pheasants are comfortable in the open, while grouse stay more under cover.

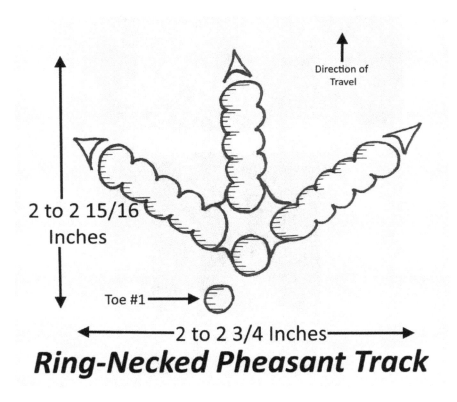

Direction of Travel

2 to 2 15/16 Inches

Toe #1 →

←————2 to 2 3/4 Inches————→

Ring-Necked Pheasant Track

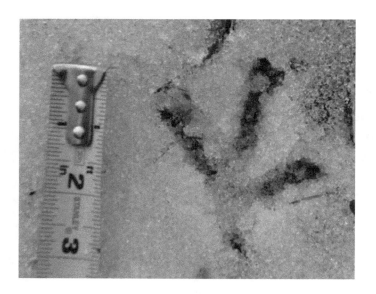

Pheasant scat

Personal Tracking Record:

Front Track ☐   Hind Track ☐   Scat ☐

Other Sign Found: _____

Date Found: _____

Habitat Found: _____

Place Found: _____

Parent's Initials: _____

Personal Tracking Record:

Front Track ☐   Hind Track ☐   Scat ☐

Other Sign Found: _____

Date Found: _____

Habitat Found: _____

Place Found: _____

Parent's Initials: _____

Personal Tracking Record:

Front Track ☐   Hind Track ☐   Scat ☐

Other Sign Found: _____

Date Found: _____

Habitat Found: _____

Place Found: _____

Parent's Initials: _____

 American White Pelican

Pelecanus erythrorhynchos

The American White Pelican is a large bird that measures from 50 to 70 inches long including the 11.3 to 15.2 inches of beak. It has a wingspan measuring between 95 to 120 inches. Males appear almost identical to females other than they are larger in size. The weigh between 7 and 30 pounds. Their feathers are bright white except the black primary and secondary remiges which are usually only visible in flight.

The American white pelican has a huge bill which is flat on top with a large throat sac below. During the breeding season, the American white pelican grows a flattened length wise horn on their bill, a couple inches from the tip. After the pelicans have mated and laid their eggs this horn is shed. When not in the breeding season, the bare skin on their feet, bill pouch and facial skin loses it's bright coloring and becomes dull.

During the breeding season, the American white pelicans are **monogamous,** having only one mate. The American white pelican courts with parallel strutting walks, head swaying and bowing along with circular courtship flights. Once a pair is formed the male will guard the female. Mating occurs from March until early May. The pair will defend a ground nest. They will nest in colonies from a few pairs to several hundred and the entire colony will build their nests during the same week. These nests become a small territory that the pair will defend by jabbing at their neighbors. These colonies are mixed with other species of birds as well.

The nests are a shallow depression scraped on the ground and can vary from bare ground, to a slight depression to a sizable mound of debris and dirt collected near the nest site. They will use sticks, twigs, and reeds to make these nests that measure between 2 and 3 feet. The American white pelican lays 1 to 3 eggs measuring 90 millimeters long and 56 millimeters wide. They are oval to long oval in shape. The shell is rough will calcareous deposits that will flake off. The eggs are dull white, smeared with blood, and nest stained and dirty. Both the male and female incubate the eggs for about one month starting when the first egg is laid.

Did you know?
Pelicans feed their chicks by re-gurgitating the fish they eat into their chicks' beak!
Gross!

The chicks are fed by regurgitation by both parents. They will leave the nest 3 to 4 weeks after hatching. The chicks will spend the next month growing their mature **plumage**, flight feathers, and learning to fly from a pond close to their nest. After **fledging**, learning to fly, the parents continue to care for their chicks about 3 more weeks until the family bond is broken in late summer or early fall. At this time the birds gather in large groups in rich feeding grounds in preparation for migration.

White Pelican Territory
IUCN Red List (2019)

The American white pelicans will spend their winter in coastal areas such as bays and estuaries. They migrate north to breed in the prairie regions of the United States and Canada on islands or near shallow inland lakes, rivers and marshes.

The American white pelican does not dive for fish, like the brown pelican. It catches its prey while swimming on the surface and dipping their bill into the water scooping up fish in their pouch. It will hunt in groups of a dozen or more to cooperatively and corral fish to one another.

Did you know?
American white pelicans eat 4
pounds of food each day?

Pelicans primarily eat fish like carp, tui chub and skinners. Each pelican eats more than four pounds of food a day. The birds also practice **kleptoparasitism,** stealing food on occasion from other birds.

The American white pelican tracks measure 6 ½ to 7 ½ Inches long and 4 ¼ to 5 3/8 inches in width. The metatarsal tends to show, webbing will inconsistently be seen in the track. The walking stride measures from 9 to 16 ½ inches.

American White Pelican

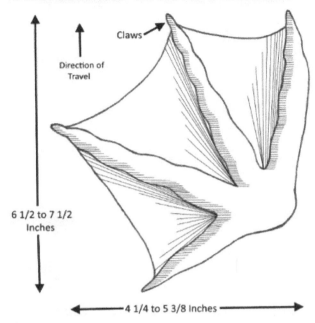

Claws

Direction of Travel

6 1/2 to 7 1/2 Inches

4 1/4 to 5 3/8 Inches

Personal Tracking Record:

Front Track ☐   Hind Track ☐   Scat ☐

Other Sign Found: _____

Date Found: _____

Habitat Found: _____

Place Found: _____

Parent's Initials: _____

Personal Tracking Record:

Front Track ☐   Hind Track ☐   Scat ☐

Other Sign Found: _____

Date Found: _____

Habitat Found: _____

Place Found: _____

Parent's Initials: _____

Personal Tracking Record:

Front Track ☐   Hind Track ☐   Scat ☐

Other Sign Found: _____

Date Found: _____

Habitat Found: _____

Place Found: _____

Parent's Initials: _____

🐾 California Quail

Callipepla californica

Male California quail

The California quail is a small ground-dwelling bird. The male has a gray chest with a brown back and wings, a black throat with white stripes, and a brown cap on his head. The hen has a gray or brown head and back with a lighter speckled chest and belly. Both the male and the female have a curved crown plume made of six feathers that stands up straight from their forehead. The male's crown feather is larger than the females.

The California quail usually eats seeds but will also eat plant parts like buds and sometimes insects. They feed in flocks in the early morning. Their habitat consists of grasslands, woodlands, canyons, and the edge of deserts. They prefer areas with a lot of brush. The California quail will roost in trees to avoid danger and to rest. If scared by a predator the quail will fly a short distance in a fast, low flight. The California quail will rarely move more than 10 miles from where it was hatched.

California Quail Territory
IUCN Red List (2019)

One of their daily activities is a dust bath. They will select soft soil and use their underbellies to burrow downward into the soil 1 to 2 inches. They will wriggle around flapping their wings and ruffling their feathers which causes the dust to rise. They prefer sunny places.

The California quail lives in flocks called a **covey** made up of 10 to 200 birds in the winter. They stay in these coveys until they pair off during the mating season. Males will perch on a tree or a post and call out to claim their territory. The males will only mate with one hen.

Dad is watching over his chicks

The hen will lay between 12 to 16 cream and brown speckled eggs. The California quail nest is found under bushes, brush-piles, next to a rock or log, in a grass clump, cactus, under a haystack, or in a rock cranny. The nest is a slight hollow or scrape in the ground lined with grass or leaves. The average egg size is 31 x 24 mm. They are short and oval, often rather pointed in shape. The eggshells are thick, hard, and dotted with shades of brown. They incubate their eggs for 3 weeks. When the chicks hatch both the mother and father will care for the chicks. The chicks will leave the nest one day after hatching and can fly a short distance when 10 days old.

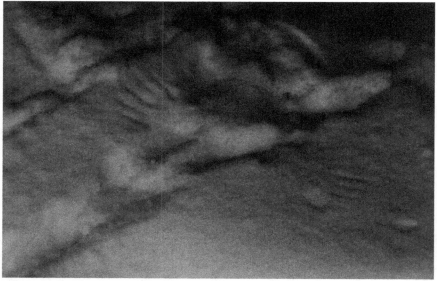

Wing tracks of California quail

The California quail's track measures 1 ¼ to 1 ½ inches in length and 1 ¼ to 1 ¾ inches wide. Toe # 1 and the metatarsal pad are usually visible. Toe #1 is the toe that goes off the back of the heel. The California quail's walking stride measures 1 ½ to 5 ½ inches (Elbroch, 2001)

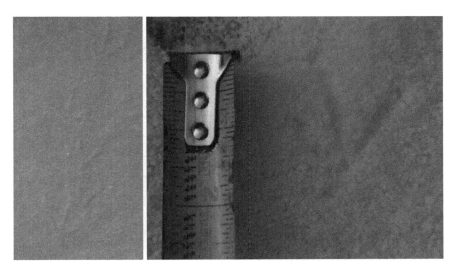

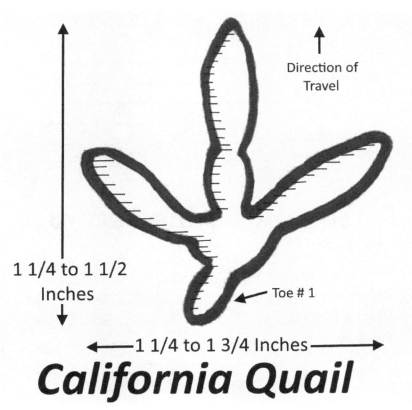

1 1/4 to 1 1/2 Inches

Direction of Travel

Toe # 1

←——1 1/4 to 1 3/4 Inches——→

California Quail

Personal Tracking Record:

Front Track ☐   Hind Track ☐   Scat ☐

Other Sign Found: _____

Date Found: _____

Habitat Found: _____

Place Found: _____

Parent's Initials: _____

Personal Tracking Record:

Front Track ☐   Hind Track ☐   Scat ☐

Other Sign Found: _____

Date Found: _____

Habitat Found: _____

Place Found: _____

Parent's Initials: _____

Personal Tracking Record:

Front Track ☐   Hind Track ☐   Scat ☐

Other Sign Found: _____

Date Found: _____

Habitat Found: _____

Place Found: _____

Parent's Initials: _____

 Mallard Duck

Anas platyrhynchos

The mallard duck's habitat is throughout the temperate and subtropical Americas. The mallard is considered waterfowl. They are strongly migratory in the northern parts of their breeding range. They prefer to live in wetlands. They eat water plants and small animals. They can adapt to a wide climate range from the arctic tundra to subtropical regions. They are found in both fresh and saltwater wetlands. They prefer a water depth of less than 3 feet, with aquatic vegetation.

Mallard Duck Territory
IUCN Red List (2019)

Males are known as drakes. They have a glossy green head and are grey on the wings and belly. The Females are known as hens. They are mainly brown with speckled plumage. This brown ranges from buff to dark brown. They have buff cheeks. They have brown eyes, with the throat and neck buff brown and a darker crown on the head and an eye stripe. Both sexes have an area of white bordered black speculum feathers which commonly also include iridescent blue feathers. Drakes have a purple tinged brown breast, and the rear of the drake is black. They have a dark tail with a white border, their bill is yellow.

Mallards are medium-sized waterfowl. They measure between 20 and 26 inches long with a wingspan between 32 and 39 inches wide. Mallards are social animals and will congregate in groups or flocks of varying sizes. They will interbreed with other species of ducks like the American black drake.

Mallards' life expectancy is 3 years but occasionally they can live to 20 years. Their ducklings begin to fly between 3 and 4 months. You can tell they are ready to fly when they have the blue speculum feathers. They are mature between 6 and 10 months.

Mallards are **omnivores**. They are very flexible in their choice. Their diet varies depending on breeding cycle stage, varieties of food available, the nutrient availability and the competition. The majority of what they eat consists of snails, insects, worms, and various seeds and plant materials, roots, and tubers. The majority of their diet is usually 60% plant material with the exception of laying hens, whose diet is 70% animal matter. Mallards forage in water by **dabbling**, submerging in water with their head down and rear up while grazing on underwater plants.

In the northern hemisphere mallards usually form breeding pairs in October and November. They stay in these pairs until the hen can lay eggs at the start of the nesting season around the beginning of spring. At this time the drakes leave their mate and join with other drakes to await the molting season which begins in June. The nesting period is rough on the hens because they lay more than half of her body weight in eggs. They require a lot of rest and feeding in an area that is safe from predators. When seeking out a nesting site, hens prefer well-concealed areas that are inaccessible to ground predators. They lay clutches of 8 to 13 eggs that will incubate for 27 to 28 days. The ducklings are fully capable of swimming as soon as they hatch. Due to the filial imprinting from the mother on the duckling, the ducklings instinctively stay near the mother for warmth and protection but also to learn about and remember their habitat as well as how to find food. When ducklings mature into flight-capable juveniles, they learn from their mother the traditional migrating routes. They will stay with their mother learning this route until the next breeding season.

Mallard tracks show 3 toes. They usually show marks from their toenails. Webbing between the toes does not always show up. The tracks measure between 2 3/8 and 2 15/16 inches in length and 2 ¼ to 3 1/16 inches wide. Toe # 1 is often seen; this is a toe that appears to go off the back of the heel. The mallard walking stride measures between 3 ¾ and 7 ½ inches (Elbroch, 2001)

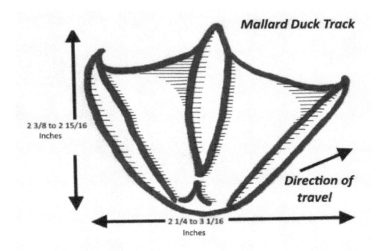

The mallard duck walks with its feet pointed slightly in toward each other as shown here.

The mallard duck nest is usually found within a half mile of water. These nests are well concealed in dense vegetation, preferably about 2 feet high. The nest is made in a depression in the ground built up with cattails, reeds, grasses, and other surrounding vegetation. Downy feathers are added sparingly until just before completion of the clutch. When the clutch, all the eggs laid during the season, is completed, the female will pluck down from her breast and use it to form a ring around the eggs. She lays between 6 and 15 eggs with an average size is 58x 42 mm. They are long oval in shape. The shell is smooth with very little luster. The eggs are light green, light gray or nearly white and unmarked.

This mallard's nest has just hatched its ducklings

Personal Tracking Record:
Front Track ☐   Hind Track ☐   Scat ☐

Other Sign Found: _____
Date Found: _____
Habitat Found: _____
Place Found: _____
Parent's Initials: _____

Personal Tracking Record:
Front Track ☐   Hind Track ☐   Scat ☐

Other Sign Found: _____
Date Found: _____
Habitat Found: _____
Place Found: _____
Parent's Initials: _____

Personal Tracking Record:
Front Track ☐   Hind Track ☐   Scat ☐

Other Sign Found: _____
Date Found: _____
Habitat Found: _____
Place Found: _____
Parent's Initials: _____

 Canada Goose

Branta canadensis

The Canada goose is a large goose with a black head and neck and a white patch on the throat up to the cheeks. They range from 30 to 43 inches in length with a 50 to 73-inch wingspan. They weigh between 5.7 and 14.3 pounds. The female looks almost identical but is a little lighter in weight, between 5.3 and 12.1 pounds. The average lifespan is between 10 and 24 years.

The Canada goose is native to the arctic and temperate regions of North America. They tend to be found on or close to fresh water. They have been successful in adapting to human habitation especially parks and cultivated areas. They are naturally migratory with their winter range being most of the United States. They will call, known as honking, while migrating and flying in their V formation. This often signals the seasonal changes to spring and autumn.

Canadian Goose Territory
IUCN Red List (2019)

The Canada goose is primarily an herbivore eating green vegetation and grains such as rice, wheat, and corn, but it will on occasions eat insects and fish. In the water, it will feed from the silt on the bottom of the pond but will also feed on seaweed.

During the second year of their lives, the Canada goose will find a mate. They are monogamous, and most stay together their whole lives. If one of the pair dies, the other may find a new mate. The female will lay between two and nine eggs with an average being five. Although both parents will protect the nest while the eggs incubate, the mother spends more time on the nest than the father. The nest is usually found in an elevated area near fresh water. This nest is usually a shallow depression lined with plant material and down. Incubation is about a month long. While the mothers incubate the eggs the father will still stay nearby. As soon as the goslings hatch, they are capable of walking swimming, and finding their own food. They are often seen walking in a line with one parent in the front and the other in the back of the goslings. While protecting the goslings the parents will violently chase away any living creature nearby. They will give a hissing warning, then bite and flap wings at the offender. The goslings do not leave the parents until the spring migration, after the parents teach their young the migration routes.

During migration, the Canada goose has staging areas where it will meet up with other flocks. They fly with their distinct V formation at an altitude of around 3,000 feet. Some geese are known to return to the same nesting sites year after year to lay their eggs with their mate.

The Canada goose tracks are between 3 7/8 and 4 3/4 inches in length from the tip of the middle toe to the heel and 3 ¾ to 5 inches wide. The middle toe is longer than the 2 side toes. They have claws that usually show in the track at the end of each toe. Their stride tracks are pointed inward and measures 3 ½ to 11 inches (Elbroch, 2001)

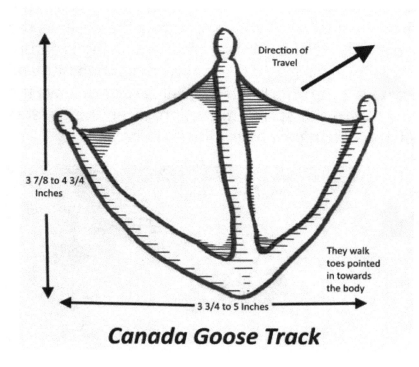

Canada Goose Track

Did you know?
Canada geese poop
1 to 3 pounds of poop
(scat) per day.
Holy Scat!!

Canadian Goose scat is typically sausage shaped. Fresh droppings are greenish and coated with white nitrogenous deposits.

The Canada goose nest is usually found near water, often on a low stump, a mound, or a muskrat house. They are found in bulrushes, reeds, and cattails and typically are a depression lined with sticks, cattails, reeds, and grasses. They are also lined with soft gray down plucked from the female's breast after she has begun laying. The outside diameter of the nest measures between 15 and 37 inches. The inside diameter measures between 6 and 13 inches. The depth of the nest measures 3 ½ to 4 ½ inches. They lay between four and seven eggs, with an average size of 86 x 58 mm. The eggs are oval to long oval. The eggshell is smooth or slightly rough with no gloss. They are creamy white or dirty white in color without any spots or speckles.

Personal Tracking Record:
Front Track ☐   Hind Track ☐   Scat ☐

Other Sign Found: _____
Date Found: _____
Habitat Found: _____
Place Found: _____
Parent's Initials: _____

Personal Tracking Record:
Front Track ☐   Hind Track ☐   Scat ☐

Other Sign Found: _____
Date Found: _____
Habitat Found: _____
Place Found: _____
Parent's Initials: _____

Personal Tracking Record:
Front Track ☐   Hind Track ☐   Scat ☐

Other Sign Found: _____
Date Found: _____
Habitat Found: _____
Place Found: _____
Parent's Initials: _____

🐾 Great Blue Heron

Ardea herodias

The great blue heron is a large wading bird that is common near the shores of open water and in wetlands over most of North America and Central America. They are found as far north as Alaska and the southern Canadian provinces during the summer months. Great Blue Herons are found further north than most other herons, even where the majority of the water freezes. During the winter they are found in the south in Florida, Mexico and down to South America. The great blue heron is the largest North American heron. It has a head-to-tail length of 36 to 54 inches, a wingspan of 66 to 79 inches, a height of 45 to 54 inches and a weight of 4 to 7.9 pounds.

Great Blue Heron Territory
IUCN Red List (2019)

The great blue heron is a slate gray with a slight blue flight feathers, red-brown thighs and a paired red-brown and black stripe up the flanks. Its neck is rusty gray with black and white streaking down the front. The head is slightly paler with a nearly white face. It has a pair of black or slate plumes that run from just above the eye to the back of the head. Its bill is dull yellow which becomes orange for the brief period during mating season.

The heron's walking stride measures around 8.7 inches in almost a straight line. All of the toes show small talons. Two of the three front toes are generally closer together.

The great blue heron is very adaptable and can adjust to almost any wetland habitat in its range. It can be found in fresh and saltwater marshes, mangrove swamps, flooded meadows, lake edges and shorelines. It can be found in developed areas as long as the water has fish. Great blue hersons can also be found in farmer's fields.

Great blue herons rarely travel far from bodies of water. They usually nest in trees or bushes near the water's edge, on islands or in isolated spots to protect from predators.

Great blue herons primarily eat small fish. They are also an opportunistic predator and will eat crabs, shrimp, aquatic insects, rodents and other small mammals, amphibians, reptiles and birds. Herons locate their prey by sight and usually swallow it whole. They are typically a solitary feeder and have been known to choke on food that is too large. They can be found hunting both during the day and night.

The great blue heron usually breeds in colonies, in trees close to water, lakes or other wetlands. They generally return to the breeding colonies from December to March, depending on the weather and how far north the breeding colonies are. These nesting colonies called **rookeries**, may have from 5 nests to 500 nests per colony. The average is 160 nests. These sites are usually difficult to reach on foot because they are islands and on trees in swamps. These colonies are usually located within 2 1/2 to 3 miles of water.

The herons are **monogamous** during the breeding season, having only one mate; however, during the next breeding season, they will get a new mate. Males arrive on the nests first and settle on a nest site to court the females. Most males will choose a new nest each year. Their nests are a bulky stick nest measuring

20 inches across when first built. They can grow to more than 47 inches in width and 35 inches deep with re-use year after year and additional construction. The female will primarily build the nest while the male brings building material.

The female will lay three to six pale blue eggs. Eggs can measure from 2 to 3 inches in length and 1.14 to 1.99 inches in width. One clutch is raised each year. The eggs are laid between March and April. The eggs are laid at a two-day interval and incubated for 27 days. The males incubate for about 10.5 hours each day while the females incubate for the rest of the day and night.

Both parents feed the young at the nest by regurgitating the food for their chicks. The first chick to hatch becomes more experienced in handling food and can become more aggressive with its siblings. After about 55 to 80 days the young herons take their first flight. They return to the nest to be fed for up to the next 3 weeks while they are being taught to catch their own prey. They gradually leave the nest during the next winter.

Their nests are generally in colonies called a rookery. It is not uncommon to have nests of other species of heron in the same colonies. There are often multiple nests in one tree. They will also nest in bushes, rock ledges, sea cliffs, and on the ground. Nests are a platform of large sticks, lined with fine twigs and green leaves. The male brings the material to the female who builds the nest. The outer measuring diameter is between 25 and 40 inches. There are usually 3 to 6 eggs, oval to long oval. The shell is smooth or slightly rough, pale bluish green, and is unmarked.

Great blue heron tracks measure 6 ½ to 8 ½ inches in length and 4 to 6 inches in width. There is some webbing present between toes 3 and 4. Toes are slim and an even width (Elbroch, 2001)

Their walking stride measures: 10 to 18 ½ inches.

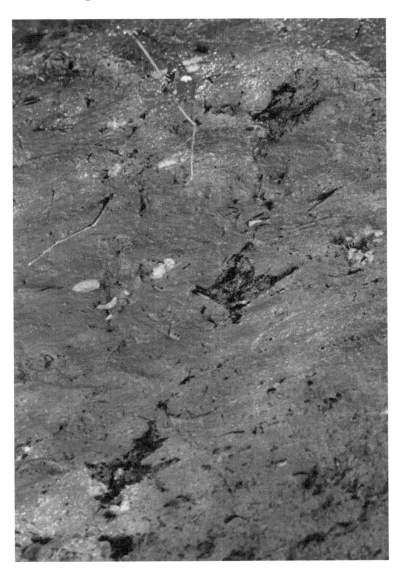

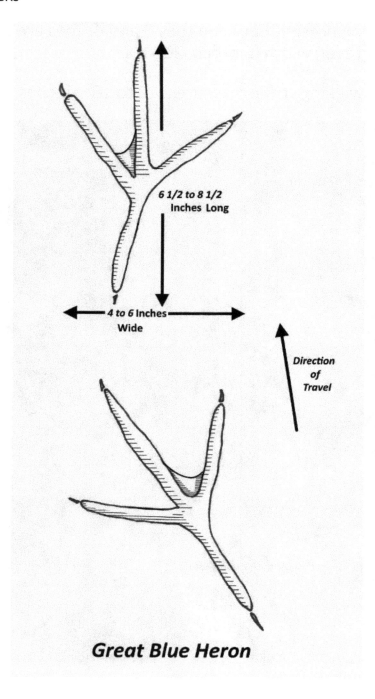

6 1/2 to 8 1/2
Inches Long

4 to 6 Inches
Wide

Direction
of
Travel

Great Blue Heron

Personal Tracking Record:

Front Track ☐   Hind Track ☐   Scat ☐

Other Sign Found: _____
Date Found: _____
Habitat Found: _____
Place Found: _____
Parent's Initials: _____

Personal Tracking Record:

Front Track ☐   Hind Track ☐   Scat ☐

Other Sign Found: _____
Date Found: _____
Habitat Found: _____
Place Found: _____
Parent's Initials: _____

Personal Tracking Record:

Front Track ☐   Hind Track ☐   Scat ☐

Other Sign Found: _____
Date Found: _____
Habitat Found: _____
Place Found: _____
Parent's Initials: _____

So next time you are about and you notice some scratches, piles of grass, or toe marks in the sand, look at the clues around you, play detective, and investigate who left the signs and what they were up to. They may just be watching you.

Answer Key

Scat and Track Identification Games

Match the Scat!

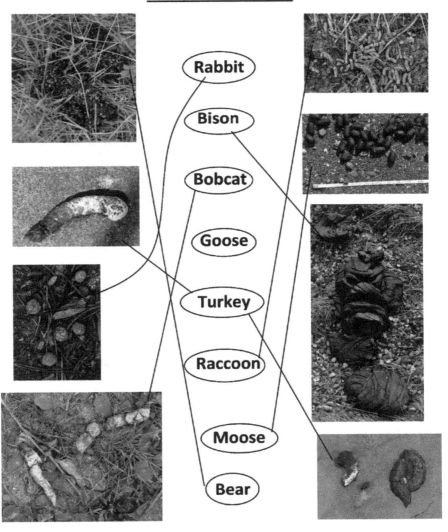

Rabbit

Bison

Bobcat

Goose

Turkey

Raccoon

Moose

Bear

How Many Can You Identify?

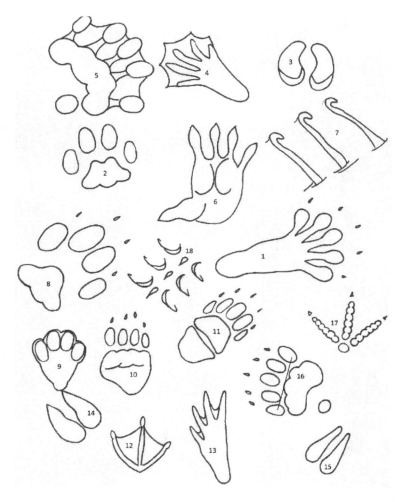

1.	Raccoon	7.	Sidewinding Snake
2.	Bobcat	8.	Coyote
3.	Bison	9.	Snowshoe Hare
4.	Beaver	10.	Porcupine
5.	Otter	11.	Striped Skunk
6.	Opossum	12.	Goose

13.	Alligator
14.	Mountain Goat
15.	Pronghorn
16.	Black Bear
17.	Turkey
18.	Green Sea Turtle

Seek and Find

Can You find: Toad Hind Track, Pheasant, Great Blue Heron, Hooded Skunk Hind Track, Bighorn Sheep Track, Grizzly bear front track, Cottontail rabbit hind tracks.

Can You Name Animal Groups? Key

Bears: sleuth or sloth
Wolves: pack, (on the move) a route or rout
Coyote: band
Fox: a skulk, leash, troop, or earth
Bighorn sheep: herd
Mountain Goat: bands
Bison: gang or obstinacy
Moose: herd
Caribou: harems
Pronghorn antelope: band or herd
Deer: (bucks)- clash, herd or stag herd
Elk: herd or gang
Wild boar: (older group) sounder, drift or drove (younger group)
Snoeshoe hare: warren
Mountain Cottontail: warren
Pika: family group
Beaver: colony or family
Hooded skunk: a stench
Striped skunk: a stench

Porcupine: a prickle
River otter: family, romp or raft
Raccoon: gaze
Badger: a cete
Opossum: passel
Prairie Dog: colonies or coteries
Squirrel: a dray or scurry
Cougar: range
Bobcat: clowder, clutter, pounce
Turtle: a bale or nest
Bullfrog: an army
Toad: a knot
Rattlesnake: a nest, rhumba
Turkey: a gang or raft
Pheasant: nest, (a brood) nide, nye
Pelican: pods or squadron
Quail: Covey or bevy
Chipmunk: scurry
Mallard duck: brace or sord
Goose: flock, gaggle (ground), skein
Heron: a sedge or siege

 Glossary

Anatomy: a study of the structure or internal workings of something.

Amble: a fast walk where the hind footprint registers behind the front footprint.

Aquatic plants: a plant that grows in water.

Bifurcated: divided into two branches or forks.

Billy goat: a male goat.

Boar: a male bear or male pig.

Bound: A gait in which both feet strike the ground at the same time, side by side.

Brumation: a state or condition of sluggishness, inactivity, or torpor exhibited by reptiles.

Cache: food in a secure or hidden storage place.

Camouflage: an adaptation that allows animals to blend in with certain aspects of their environment.

Carapace: the hard upper-shell of a turtle.

Cervid: a mammal of the deer family.

Clout: toes #3 and #4 of the hoof, the larger 2 toes.

Communal Denning: the lair or shelter of a wild animal shared by all members of a community.

Convergence Zones: a location where ocean currents meet, characteristically marked by downwelling of water.

Crepuscular: appearing or active in twilight-type lighting, such as dawn.

Dabbling: submerging in water with their head down and their tails up while grazing on underwater plants.

Dew claw: a digit, vestigial in some animals.

Deciduous forest: vegetation composed primarily of broad leaved trees that shed all their leaves during one season.

Direct register: a track where the hind foot lands on where the front foot had been.

Diurnal: during the day.

Ectotherm: an animal that is dependent on external sources of body heat.

Ewe: a female sheep.

Forage: an animal searching widely for food or provisions.

Gait: Types of movement an animal uses when moving.

Gallop: a gait where the hind feet move around the front feet and strike the ground in front of the front feet.

Gestation: the process of carrying or being carried in the womb between conception and birth, pregnancy.

Group: a subunit of a stride including four footprints from the four feet of an animal.

Gular fold: a granular fold found on the ventral throat located immediately in front of the forelegs; for alligators and crocodiles the function is to prevent the water from entering the trachea when the alligator has the mouth open under water.

Hibernaculum: a shelter occupied during the winter by a dormant animal.

Jake: a sexually immature male wild turkey.

Keratin: fibrous structural protein of hair, nails, hoofs, wool, feathers and of the epithelial cells in the outer most layer of skin.

Keystone species: a species on which other species in an ecosystem largely depend, such that if it were removed the ecosystem would change drastically.

Kleptoparasitism: parasitism by theft, a form of feeding in which one animal takes prey or other food that was caught by another animal.

Lateral: of, at, toward, or from the side or sides.

Lope: a slow gallop in which at least one hind foot registers behind a front foot in a group of four footprints.

Marsupial: a mammal of an order whose members are born incompletely developed and are typically carried and nursed in a pouch on the mother's belly.

Migrate: when an animal moves from one region or habitat to another according to the season.

Molt: shed old feathers, hair, or skin, or an old shell, to make way for new growth.

Monogamous: having only one mate at a time.

Nanny goat: a female goat.

Natal homing: the process by which some adult animals return to their birthplace to reproduce.

Nictitating membrane: translucent membrane that forms an inner eye lid in birds, reptiles and some mammals. It can be drawn across the eye to protect it from dust and keep it moist.

Nest parasitism: one bird will lay their eggs in another bird's nest. The bird who has the nest ends up raising the first bird's chick.

Nocturnal: active at night.

Non-perishable: not readily subjected to spoilage or decay.

Nomadic: wandering.

Omnivore – an animal or person that eats food of both plant and animal origin.

Overstep Track: a track where the hind foot lands beyond where the front foot had been.

Palmate: an antler in which the angles between the tines are partly filled in to form a broad flat surface.

Pelagic: inhabiting the upper layers of the open sea.

Plastron: the ventral, (under) part of a shell of a tortoise or turtle typically of nine symmetrically placed bones overlaid by horny plates.

Polygamous: typically having more than one mate.

Poult: a turkey chick.

Prehensile: capable of grasping.

Pronk: a leap in the air with an arched back and stiff legs.

Ram: male sheep.

Rookery: a breeding colony of rooks, typically seen as a collection of nests.

Roosting: bird or bats, settle or congregate for rest or sleep.

Ruminant: an even toed ungulate mammal that chews the cud regurgitated from its rumen. The ruminants comprise the cattle, sheep, antelope, deer, giraffe and their relatives.

Scutes: a thickened horny or bony plate on a turtles shell or on the back of a crocodile.

Semi-arboreal: often inhabiting and frequenting trees but not completely living in trees.

Sounder: a herd of wild swine.

Sow: a female bear or female pig.

Stalk: pursue or approach stealthily, only one foot moves at a time.

Straddle: the distance from the right edge of the rightmost pad to the leftmost pad in a trail.

Stride: The distance from the point where a foot touches the ground to the point where the same foot touches the ground again.

Subunguis: The soft material between the pad and the wall.

Suid: a swine.

Symbiotic Relationship: a close relationship between two species in which at least one species benefits.

Temperate climate: environments with moderate rainfall spread across the year or portion of the year with sporadic drought, mild to warm summers and cool to cold winters.

Tom: adult male turkey.

Trot: a gait in which evenly spaced footprints alternate on right and left sides of the line of travel. Hind footprint registers on top of the front. As speed increases the hind foot moves forward of the front foot.

Tympanum: a frog's tympanic membrane, or tympanum is the circular patch of skin directly behind it's eye that we commonly call it's eardrum.

Understep: track from a stalking animal, the front track.

Unguis: hard material forming hoof walls in deer and their relatives.

Ungulate: a hoofed animal.

Vibrissae: long stiff hairs growing around the mouth or elsewhere on the face of many mammals, used as organs of touch: whiskers.

Walk: to advance or travel on foot at a moderate speed or pace.

Wallow: an area of mud or shallow water where mammals go to wallow, typically developing into a depression in the ground over long use.

Wean: to accustom an infant or young mammal to food other than its mother's milk.

 Bibliography

Airway Publishing. (2018). Turtle Detectives Turtle Tracker. Conservationtales.com/turtle-tracks.html. Downloaded on 7 February 2020

Alaska Department of Fish and Game. (1999). Oreamnos americanus. Adfg.alaska.gov/index. cfm?adfg=goat.main. Downloaded on 1 May 2020

American Expedition. (2015). North American Beaver Information, Photos, Habitat, and Facts. Forum. americanexpedition.us/north-america-beaver-facts-information-and-photos. Downloaded on 18 April 2020

Anderson, R. (2002). "Castor Canadensis," Animal DiversityWeb.https://animaldiversity.org/accounts /Castor_canadensis/. Downloaded on 18 April 2020

Audubon 2020. Audubon Guide to North American Birds California Quail Callipepla californica. audubon.org/field-guide/bird/California-quail. Downloaded on 3 April 2020

Audubon 2020. Audubon Guide to North American Birds Canada Goose Branta canadensis. audubon. org/field-guide/bird/canada-goose. Downloaded on 4 April 2020

Audubon 2020. Audubon Guide to North American Birds Great Blue Heron Ardea Herodias. audubon.org/field-guide/bird/great-blue-heron. Downloaded on 3 April 2020

Audubon. Audubon Guide to North American Birds Mallard Anas platyrhynchos. audubon.org/field-guide/bird/mallard. Downloaded on 4 April 2020

Audubon. Audubon Guide to North American Birds Ring-necked Pheasant Phasianus colchicus. audubon.org/field-guide/bird/ring-necked-pheasant. Downloaded on 5 April 2020

Audubon. Audubon Guide to North American Birds Ruffed Grouse Bonasa umbellus. audubon.org/field-guide/bird/ruffed-grouse. Downloaded on 5 April 2020

Audubon. Audubon Guide to North American Birds Wild Turkey Meleagris gallopavo. audubon.org/field-guide/bird/wild-turkey. Downloaded on 5 April 2020

Aune, K., Jørgensen, D. & Gates, C. (2017). Bison bison (errata version published in 2018). The IUCN Red List of Threatened Species 2017: e.T2815A123789863. http://dx.doi.org/10.2305/IUCN.UK.2017-3.RLTS.T2815A45156541.en. Downloaded on 16 December 2019

Bairos-Novak, K. (2014). "Mephitis macroura," Animal Diversity Web. https://animaldiversity.org/accounts/Mephitis_macroura/. Downloaded on 17 April 2020

Ballenger, L. (1999). "Ovis Canadensis," Animal DiversityWeb.https://animaldiversity.org/accounts/Ovis_canadensis/. Downloaded on 19 April 2020

Bartalucci, A. and B. Weinstein. (2000). "Alces americanus," Animal Diversity Web. https://animaldiversity.org/accounts/Alces_americanus/. Downloaded on 18 April 2020

Bauer, E. (1995). Elk Behaviors, Ecology, and Conservation. Stillwater, MN. Voyager Press Inc

BirdLife International 2017. Anas platyrhynchos (amended version of 2016 assessment). The IUCN Red List of Threatened Species 2017: e.T22680186A119275821. http://dx.doi.org/10.2305/IUCN.UK.2017-3.RLTS.T22680186A119275821.en. Downloaded on 16 December 2019

BirdLife International 2016. Ardea herodias. The IUCN Red List of Threatened Species 2016: e.T22696998A93597223. http://dx.doi.org/10.2305/IUCN.UK.2016-3.RLTS.T22696998A93597223.en. Downloaded on 16 December 2019

BirdLife International 2018. Bonasa umbellus. The IUCN Red List of Threatened Species 2018: e.T22679500A131905854. Downloaded on 16 December 2019

BirdLife International 2018. Branta canadensis. The IUCN Red List of Threatened Species 2018:e. T22679935A131909406. http://dx.doi.org /10.2305/IUCN.UK.2018-2.RLTS.T22679935A 131909406.en. Downloaded on 16 December 2019

BirdLife International 2018. Callipepla californica. The IUCN Red List of Threatened Species 2018:e. T22679603A131906420. http://dx.doi.org /10.2305/IUCN.UK.2018-2.RLTS.T22679603A 131906420.en. Downloaded on 16 December 2019

BirdLife International. 2016. Pelecanus erythrorhynchos. The IUCN Red List of Threatened Species 2016: e.T22697611A93624242. https:// dx.doi.org/10.2305/IUCN.UK.2016-3.RLTS.T22697 611A93624242.en. Downloaded on 30 June 2020

BirdLife International 2016. Phasianus colchicus. The IUCN Red List of Threatened Species 2016: e.T45100023A85926819. http://dx.doi.org /10.2305/IUCN.UK.2016-3.RLTS.T45100023A8 5926819.en. Downloaded on 16 December 2019

BirdLife International 2018. Meleagris gallopavo. The IUCN Red List of Threatened Species

2018:e.T22679525A132051953.http://dx.doi.org/10.2305/IUCN.UK.2018-2.RLTS.T22679525A132051953.en. Downloaded on 16 December 2019.\

Blair, Gerry. (2007). Predator Calling. Iola, WI. Krause Publications

Boitani, L., Phillips, M. & Jhala, Y. (2018). Canis lupus . The IUCN Red List of Threatened Species 2018: e.T3746A119623865. http://dx.doi.org/10.2305/IUCN.UK.2018-2.RLTS.T3746A119623865.en. Downloaded on 16 December 2019

Breening, Sandra. (2020). University of Michigan Museum of Zoology. Lithobates catesblianus American Bullfrog. Animaldiversity.org/accounts/Lithobates_catesbeianus/. Downloaded on 7 April 2020

Brook, S.M., Pluháček, J., Lorenzini, R., Lovari, S., Masseti, M., Pereladova, O. & Mattioli, S. (2018). Cervus canadensis (errata version published in 2019). The IUCN Red List of Threatened Species 2018: e.T55997823A142396828. http://dx.doi.org/10.2305/IUCN.UK.2018-2.RLTS.T55997823A142396828.en. Downloaded on 20 December 2019

Burke Museum. Western Toad Anaxyrus boreas. Burkemuseum.org/collections-and-research/biology/

herpetology/amphibians-reptiles-washington/western-toad

Byers, J. (2003). Built for Speed, A Year in the Life of Pronghorn. Cambridge, MA. Harvard University Press

Cabrera, Kim. (2018). Western toad Bufo boreas. Bear-tracker. www.bear-tracker.com/toad.html. Retrieved on 9/8/2019

Calef, G. (1995). Caribou and the Barren Lands. Ottawa, Ontario. Firefly Books

Cassola, F. (2016). Castor canadensis. The IUCN Red List of Threatened Species 2016: e.T4003A22187946. http://dx.doi.org/10.2305/IUCN.UK.2016-3. RLTS.T4003A22187946.en. Downloaded on 16 December 2019

Cassola, F. (2016). Cynomys ludovicianus (errata version published in 2017). The IUCN Red List of Threatened Species 2016: e.T6091A115080297. http://dx.doi.org/10.2305/IUCN.UK.2016-3. RLTS.T6091A22261137.en. Downloaded on 16 December 2019

Cassola, F. (2016). Neotamias minimus (errata version published in 2017). The IUCN Red List of Threatened Species 2016: e.T42572A115190804. http://dx.doi.org/10.2305/IUCN.UK.2016-3.

RLTS.T42572A22267269.en. Downloaded on 16 December 2019

Cat Specialist Group 2002. Lynx rufus. The IUCN Red List of Threatened Species 2002: e.T12521A3352960. Downloaded on 16 December 2019

Cornell Lab (2019). All About Birds California Quail Identification. allaboutbirds.org/guide/california_Quail/id. Downloaded on 3 April 2020

Cornell Lab (2019). All About Birds Canada Goose Identification. allaboutbirds.org/guide/canada_goose/id. Downloaded on 4 April 2020

Cornell Lab (2019). All about Birds Great Blue Heron Identification. allaboutbirds.org/guide/great_blue_heron/id. Downloaded on 3 April 2020

Cornell Lab (2019). All About Birds Mallard Duck Identification. allaboutbirds.org/guide/mallard/id. Downloaded on 4 April 2020

Cornell Lab (2019). All About Birds Ring-necked Pheasant Identification. allaboutbirds.org/guide/bird/ring-necked pheasant. Downloaded on 5 April 2020

Cornell Lab (2019). All about Birds Ruffed Grouse Identification. allaboutbirds.org/guide/

Ruffed_Grouse/overview. Downloaded on 5 April 2020

Cornell Lab (2019). All About Birds Wild Turkey Identification.allaboutbirds.org/guide/Wild_Turkey /id. Downloaded on 5 April 2020

Cuarón, A.D., González-Maya, J.F., Helgen, K., Reid, F., Schipper,J.&Dragoo,J.W.(2016).Mephitismacroura. The IUCN Red List of Threatened Species 2016: e.T41634A45211135. http://dx.doi.org/10.2305/ IUCN.UK.2016-1.RLTS.T41634A45211135.en. Downloaded on 20 December 2019

Dewey, T. (2003). "Odocoileus virginianus," Animal DiversityWeb.https://animaldiversity.org/accounts /Odocoileus_virginianus/. Downloaded on 19 April 2020

Dewey, T. 2009. "Pelecanus erythrorhynchos" (On-line), Animal Diversity Web. Accessed June 27, 2020 at https://animaldiversity.org/accounts/ Pelecanus_erythrorhynchos/

Dohring, A. (2002). Animal Diversity. Sylvilagus nuttallii Mountain Cottontail. Animaldiversity.org/ accounts/sylvilagus_nuttallii. Downloaded on 5 April 2020

Elbroch, M. (2001). Bird Tracks and Sign. China. Stackpole Books

Elbroch, M. (2003). Mammal Tracks and Sign. China. Stackpole Books

Ellis, E. 2003. "Lontra canadensis," Animal Diversity Web. https://animaldiversity.org/accounts/Lontra_canadensis/. Downloaded on 14 April 2020

Ellis, E.; B. Guilliams; W. Mowbray; A. Patton and S. Gloss. (2007). "Oreamnos americanus," Animal Diversity Web. https://animaldiversity.org/accounts/Oreamnos_americanus/. Downloaded on 19 April 2020

Elsey, R., Woodward, A. & Balaguera-Reina, S.A. (2019). Alligator mississippiensis. The IUCN Red List of Threatened Species 2019: e.T46583A3009637. http://dx.doi.org/10.2305/IUCN.UK.2019-2.RLTS.T46583A3009637.en. Downloaded on 16 December 2019

Emmons, L. (2016). Erethizon dorsatum. The IUCN Red List of Threatened Species 2016: e.T8004A22213161. http://dx.doi.org/10.2305/IUCN.UK.2016-3.RLTS.T8004A22213161.en. Downloaded on 16 December 2019

Evans, J. (2016). Reptile and Amphibian (Herp) Tracks and Sign. Nature Tracking. url:naturetracking.com/herp-tracks/. Retrieved on 8/23/2019

Fahey, B. (2001). "Sciurus niger," Animal Diversity Web. https://animaldiversity.org/accounts/Sciurus_niger/ Downloaded on 9 April 2020

Festa-Bianchet, M. (2008). Oreamnos americanus. The IUCN Red List of Threatened Species 2008: e.T42680A10727959. http://dx.doi.org/10.2305/IUCN.UK.2008.RLTS.T42680A10727959.en. Downloaded on 16 December 2019

Festa-Bianchet, M. 2008. Ovis canadensis. The IUCN Red List of Threatened Species 2008: e.T15735A5075259. http://dx.doi.org/10.2305/IUCN.UK.2008.RLTS.T15735A5075259.en. Downloaded on 16 December 2019

Fox, D. (2007). "Vulpes vulpes", Animal Diversity Web. https://animaldiversity.org/accounts/Vulpes_vulpes/. Downloaded on 19 April 2020

Fox, R. (2001). "Procyon lotor," Animal Diversity Web. https://animaldiversity.org/accounts/Procyon_lotor/. Downloaded on 13 April 2020

Frost, D.R., Hammerson, G.A. & Santos-Barrera, G. (2007). Crotalus viridis. The IUCN Red List of Threatened Species 2007: e.T64339A12771847. http://dx.doi.org/10.2305/IUCN.UK.2007.RLTS.T64339A12771847.en. Downloaded on 16 December 2019

Gallina, S. and Lopez Arevalo, H. (2016). Odocoileus virginianus. The IUCN Red List of Threatened Species 2016: e.T42394A22162580. http://dx.doi.org /10.2305/IUCN.UK.2016-2.RLTS.T42394A2216 2580.en. Downloaded on 16 December 2019

Garshelis, D.L., Scheick, B.K., Doan-Crider, D.L., Beecham, J.J. & Obbard, M.E. (2016). Ursus americanus (errata version published in 2017). The IUCN Red List of Threatened Species 2016: e.T41687A114251609. http://dx.doi.org/10.2305/ IUCN.UK.2016-3.RLTS.T41687A45034604.en. Downloaded on 16 December 2019

Global Invasive Species Database. (2020) Species profile: Sus scrofa. http://www.iucngisd.org/gisd/ speciesname/Sus+scrofa. Downloaded on 16 June 2020

Green Sea Turtle (Chelonia mydas). National Geographic Society. (December 29, 2005). Archived from original 2007-02-05. Downloaded on 8 February 2020

Gunn, A. (2016). Rangifer tarandus. The IUCN Red List of Threatened Species 2016: e.T29742A22167140. http://dx.doi.org/10.2305/IUCN.UK.2016-1.RLTS.T2 9742A22167140.en. Downloaded on 16 December 2019

Halfpenny, J. (2015). Scats and Tracks of the Pacific Coast. Guilford. Falconguides

Harrison, H. (1979). Western Bird's Nests. USA. Peterson Field Guides

Helgen, K. & Reid, F. (2016). Mephitis mephitis. The IUCN Red List of Threatened Species 2016: e.T41635A45211301. http://dx.doi.org/10.2305/ IUCN.UK.2016-1.RLTS.T41635A45211301.en. Downloaded on 20 December 2019

Helgen, K. & Reid, F. (2016). Taxidea taxus. The IUCN Red List of Threatened Species 2016: e.T41663A45215410. http://dx.doi.org/10.2305/ IUCN.UK.2016-1.RLTS.T41663A45215410.en. Downloaded on 16 December 2019

Hoffmann, M. & Sillero-Zubiri, C. (2016). Vulpes vulpes. The IUCN Red List of Threatened Species 2016: e.T23062A46190249. http://dx.doi.org/10.2305/ IUCN.UK.2016-1.RLTS.T23062A46190249.en. Downloaded on 16 December 2019

Horton, Jennifer. (2020). How stuff works. What's the difference between a bobcat and a lynx? Animals. howstuffworks.com/mammals/bobcat-vs-lynx. htm. Downloaded on 9 April 2020

Hundertmark, K. (2016). Alces alces. The IUCN Red List of Threatened Species 2016:

e.T56003281A22157381. http://dx.doi.org/10.2305
/IUCN.UK.2016-1.RLTS.T56003281A22157381.
en. Downloaded on 16 December 2019

IUCN SSC Amphibian Specialist Group 2015.
Anaxyrus boreas. The IUCN Red List of Threatened
Species 2015: e.T3179A53947725. http://dx.doi.
org/10.2305/IUCN.UK.2015-4.RLTS.T3179A53
947725.en. Downloaded on 16 December 2019

IUCN SSC Amphibian Specialist Group 2015.
Lithobates catesbeianus. The IUCN Red List of
Threatened Species 2015: e.T58565A53969770.
http://dx.doi.org/10.2305/IUCN.UK.2015-4.RLTS.T
58565A53969770.en. Downloaded on 16
December 2019

IUCN SSC Antelope Specialist Group 2016. Antilocapra
americana (errata version published in 2017).
The IUCN Red List of Threatened Species 2016:
e.T1677A115056938. http://dx.doi.org/10.2305/
IUCN.UK.2016-3.RLTS.T1677A50181848.en.
Downloaded on 16 December 2019

Kays, R. (2018). Canis latrans . The IUCN Red List of
Threatened Species 2018: e.T3745A103893556.
http://dx.doi.org/10.2305/IUCN.UK.2018-2.RLTS.T
3745A103893556.en. Downloaded on 16
December 2019

Klein, S. (1983). The Encyclopedia of North American Wildlife. Facts on File. Inc

Kobalenko, J. (1997). Forest Cats, Cougars, Bobcats, and Lynx of North America. Buffalo, NY. Firefly Books

Linzey, A.V., Timm, R., Emmons, L. & Reid, F. (2016). Sciurus niger (errata version published in 2017). The IUCN Red List of Threatened Species 2016: e.T20016A115155257. http://dx.doi.org/10.2305/IUCN.UK.2016-3.RLTS.T20016A22247226.en. Downloaded on 16 December

Maryland Department of Natural Resources. (2018). The Secretive Wild Feline: A Profile Of A Bobcat in Maryland. News.maryland.gov/dnr/2018/03/30/secretive-wild-feline/. Downloaded on 9 April 2020

Mayer, John J.; Brisbin, I. Lehr Jr. (March 1, 2008). Wild Pigs in the United States. Their History, Comparitive Morphology, and Current Status. University of Georgia Press. pp. 20ff. ISBN978-08203-3137-9. Downloaded on 8 February 2020

McClay, Robin. Citizens for the Preservation of Wildlife, Inc. About Canada Geese. Preservewildlife.com/Canada-geese.html. Downloaded on 4 April 2020

McLellan, B.N., Proctor, M.F., Huber, D. & Michel, S. (2017). Ursus arctos (amended version of 2017 assessment). The IUCN Red List of Threatened Species 2017: e.T41688A121229971. http://dx.doi.org/10.2305/IUCN.UK.2017-3.RLTS.T41688A121229971.en. Downloaded on 16 December 2019

Mills, L. & Smith, A.T. (2019). Lepus americanus. The IUCN Red List of Threatened Species 2019: e.T41273A45185466. http://dx.doi.org/10.2305/IUCN.UK.2019-1.RLTS.T41273A45185466.en. Downloaded on 16 December 2019

Misuraca, M. (19990. "Odocoileus hemionus," Animal Diversity Web. https://animaldiversity.org/accounts/Odocoileus_hemionus/. Downloaded on 18 April 2020

Morkowitz, David. 2020. Signs of Wolves. Westernwildlife.org/gray-wolf-outreach-progect/signs-of-wolves./ Downloaded on 18 February 2020

National Wildlife Federation. American Alligator. nwf.org/Educational-Resources/Wildlife-Guide/. Downloaded on 5 April 2020

Nature Raccoon Nation. (2012). Raccoon Facts. Pbs.org/wnet/nature/raccoon-nation-raccoon-fact-sheet/7553/. Downloaded on 13 April 2020

Nature Works. (2019). American Alligator-Alligator mississippiensis.PBS.www.nhptv.org/natureworks/americanalligator.htm. Retrieved on 16 December 2019

NatureWorks.(2020).BighornSheep-Oviscanadensis. PBS. nhpbs.org/natureworks/bighornsheep.htm. Downloaded on 1 May 2020

Nature Works. (2020). White-Tailed Deer. Odocoileus virginianus. PBS. www.nhpbs.org/natureworks/whitetaileddeer.htm. Downloaded on 19 April 2020

National Park Service Bighorn Canyon. (2015). Prairie Rattlesnake. Nps.gov/bica/learn/prairie-rattlesnake.htm. Downloaded on 8 April 2020

National Park Service. (2018). Bighorn Sheep. nps.gov/room/learn/nature/bighorn_sheep.htm. Downloaded on 1 May 2020

Nelson, Rob. (2020). Untamed Science Least Chipmunk Tamias minimus. Untamedscience.com/biodiversity/least-chipmunk/. Downloaded on 10 April 2020

Newell, T. and A. Sorin 2003. "Bison bison," Animal Diversity Web https://animaldiversity.org/accounts/Bison_bison/. Downloaded on 19 April 2020

Nielsen, C., Thompson, D., Kelly, M. & Lopez-Gonzalez, C.A. (2015). Puma concolor (errata version published in 2016). The IUCN Red List of Threatened Species 2015: e.T18868A97216466. http://dx.doi.org/10.2305/IUCN.UK.2015-4.RLTS.T18868A50663436.en. Downloaded on 16 December 2019

Pérez-Hernandez, R., Lew, D. & Solari, S. (2016). Didelphis virginiana. The IUCN Red List of Threatened Species 2016: e.T40502A22176259. http://dx.doi.org/10.2305/IUCN.UK.2016-1.RLTS.T40502A22176259.en. Downloaded on 16 December 2019

Peri, A. (2012). "Ochotona princeps," Animal Diversity Web. https://animaldiversity.org/accounts/Ochotona_princeps/. Downloaded on 18 April 2020

Rocky Mountain Elk Foundation. (2020). Rmef.org/elk-facts/. Downloaded on 18 April 2020

Ruffed Grouse Society. (2019). Grouse Facts. Ruffedgrousesociety.org/grouse-facts/#bio. Downloaded on 5 April 2020

Sanchez Rojas, G. and Gallina Tessaro, S. (2016). Odocoileus hemionus. The IUCN Red List of Threatened Species 2016: e.T42393A22162113. http://dx.doi.org/10.2305/IUCN.UK.2016-1.

RLTS.T42393A22162113.en. Downloaded on 16 December 2019

Savannah River Ecology Laboratory University of Georgia. American Alligator Alligator mississippiensis. Srelherp.uga.edu/alligators/allmis. htm. Downloaded on 5 April 2020

Schlimme, K. (2000). "Tamias minimus," Animal DiversityWeb.https://animaldiversity.org/accounts /Tamias_minimus/ Downloaded on 9 April 2020

Senseman, R. (2002). "Cervus elaphus," Animal DiversityWeb.https://animaldiversity.org/accounts /Cervus_elaphus/. Downloaded on 19 April 2020

Sept, J. (2017). Animal Tracks and Signs of the Northwest. Sechelt. Calypso

Serfass, T., Evans, S.S. & Polechla, P. (2015). Lontra canadensis . The IUCN Red List of Threatened Species 2015: e.T12302A21936349. http://dx.doi. org/10.2305/IUCN.UK.2015-2.RLTS.T12302A2 1936349.en. Downloaded on 16 December 2019

Sharp, Jay. (2020). Desert USA. The Badger Taxedea taxus. Desertusa.com/animals/badger.html. Downloaded on 12 April 2020

Shefferly, N. (1999). "Taxidea taxus," Animal Diversity Web. https://animaldiversity.org/accounts/Taxidea _taxus/. Downloaded on 11 April 2020

Sheldon, I. (2001). Animal Tracks of Florida, Georgia and Alabama. Auburn. Lone Pine Publishing

Siciliano, Martina, L. 2013. "Didelphis virginiana," Animal Diversity Web. https://animaldiversity.org/ accounts/Didelphis_virginiana/. Downloaded on 11 April 2020

Smith, A.T. and Beever, E. (2016). Ochotona princeps. The IUCN Red List of Threatened Species 2016: e.T41267A45184315. http://dx.doi.org/10.2305/ IUCN.UK.2016-3.RLTS.T41267A45184315.en. Downloaded on 16 December 2019

Smith, A.T. & Boyer, A.F. (2008). Sylvilagus nuttallii. The IUCN Red List of Threatened Species 2008: e.T41300A10434194. http://dx.doi.org/10.2305/ IUCN.UK.2008.RLTS.T41300A10434194.en. Downloaded on 16 December 2019

Snake Facts. (2014). Prarie Rattlesnake Crotalus Viridis. Weebly. Snake-fact.weebly.com/prairie-rattlesnake.html. Retrieved on 23 August 2019

Team, Ben. (2020). How to Tell Wolf Tracks From Dog Tracks. Dogcare.dailypuppy.com

/how-to-tell-wolf-tracks-from-dog-tracks-747 2639.html. Downloaded on 18 February 2020

Texas Tech University Natural Science Research Laboratory. (2020). Eastern Fox Squirrel Sciurus niger Linnaeus 1758. Deptsttu.edu/nsr1/mammals-of-texas-online-edition/accounts_Rodentia/ Sciurus_niger.php. Downloaded on 9 April 2020

Tkaczyk, Filip. (2015). Tracks and Sign of Reptiles and Amphibians A Guide to North American Species. Stackpole Books

Timm, R., Cuarón, A.D., Reid, F., Helgen, K. & González-Maya, J.F. (2016). Procyon lotor. The IUCN Red List of Threatened Species 2016: e.T41686A45216638. http://dx.doi.org/10.2305/IUCN.UK.2016-1.RLTS.T 41686A45216638.en. Downloaded on 16 December 2019

U.S.D.A. U.S. Department of Agriculture National Invasive Species Information Center. (2019). Aphis.usda.gov/wildlife_damage/feral_swine_ distribution-map.jpg. Downloaded on 15 June 2020

U.S. Fish and Wildlife Service. "American Pika." Downloaded on 8 February 2020

Virginia Herpetological Society. (2020). American Bullfrog Lithobates catesbeianus. Virginiaherpetologicalsociety.com/amphibians/grogs and toads/American-bullfrog/american_bullfrong. php

Wallo, O.C. (1981). Mule and Black-tailed deer distribution and habitats. Pp. 1-25, in Mule and Black-tailed deer of North America (O.C.Wallmo, ed.), Univ. Nebraska Press, Lincoln, xvii+605 pp

Weber, C. (2004). "Erethizon dorsatum," Animal DiversityWeb.https://animaldiversity.org/accounts /Erethizon_dorsatum/. Downloaded on 14 April 2020

Western Toad — Anaxyrus boreas. Montana Field Guide. Montana Natural Heritage Program and Montana Fish, Wildlife and Parks. Downloaded on 7 April 2020, from http://FieldGuide.mt.gov/ speciesDetail.aspx?elcode=AAABB01030

Wickline, K. (2014). "Sus scrofa," Animal Diversity Web. https://animaldiversity.org/accounts/Sus_ scrofa/. Downloaded on 18 April 2020

Wikipedia. (2019). American Alligator. en.wikipedia. org/wiki/American_alligator. Retrieved on 23 August 2019

Wikipedia. (2019). American Badger: en.wikipedia. org/wiki/American_badger. Retrieved on 17 February 2019

Wikipedia. (2019). American Black Bear: en.wikipedia. org/wiki/American_black_bear. Retrieved on 10 February 2019

Wikipedia. (2019). American bullfrog: en.wikipedia. org/wiki/American_bullfrog. Retrieved on 5 September 2019

Wikipedia. (2020). American white pelican: en.wikipedia.org/wiki/American_white_pelican. Retrieved on 28 June 2020

Wikipedia.(2019). Beaver: en.wikipedia.org/wiki/ Beaver. Retrieved on 17 February 2019

Wikipedia. (2019). Bighorn Sheep. en.wikipedia.org/ wiki/Bighorn_sheep. Retrieved on 15 September 2019

Wikipedia.(2019). Bison: en.wikipedia.org/wiki/Bison. Retrieved on 10 February 2019

Wikipedia. (2019). Bobcat: en.wikipedia.org/wiki/ Bobcat. Retrieved on 10 February 2019

Wikipedia. (2019). California Quail: en.wikipedia.org/ wiki/California_quail. Retrieved on 23 August 2019

Wikipedia. (2019). Canada Goose: en.wikipedia.org/ wiki/Canada_goose. Retrieved on 10 February 2019

Wikipedia. (2019). Common Pheasant: en.wikipedia. org/wiki/common_pheasant. Retrieved on 25 August 2019

Wikipedia. (2019). Cougar: en.wikipedia.org/wiki/ cougar. Retrieved on 17 February 2019

Wikipedia. (2019). Coyote: en.wikipedia.org/wiki/ coyote. Retrieved on 20 February 2019

Wikipedia. (2019). Crotalus viridis: en.wikipedia.org/ wiki/Crotalus_viridis. Retrieved on 5 September 2019

Wikipedia. (2019). Elk: en.wikipedia.org/wiki/Elk. Retrieved on 10 February 2019

Wikipedia. (2019). Fox Squirrel: en.wikipedia.org/ wiki/Fox_squirrel. Retrieved on 15 September 2019

Wikipedia. (2019). Great Blue Heron: en.wikipedia. org/wiki/Great_blue_heron. Retrieved on 2 February 2019

Wikipedia. (2020). Green Sea Turtle. en.wikipedia.org/ wiki/Green_sea_turtle. Retrieved on 7 February 2020

Wikipedia. (2019). Grizzly Bear: en.wikipedia.org/ wiki/Grizzly_bear. Retrieved on 23 August 2019

Wikipedia. (2019). Hooded Skunk: en.wikipedia.org/wiki/Hooded_skunk. Retrieved on 10 February 2019

Wikipedia. (2019). Least Chipmunk: en.wikipedia.org/wiki/Least_Chipmunk. Retrieved on 10 February 2019

Wikipedia. (2019). Mallard: en.wikipedia.org/wiki/Mallard. Retrieved on 17 February 2019

Wikipedia. (2019). Moose: en.wikipedia.org/wiki/Moose. Retrieved on 15 September 2019

Wikipedia. (2019). Mountain Goat. en.wikipedia.org/wiki/Mountian_goat. Retrieved on 15 September 2019

Wikipedia. (2019). Mule deer: en.wikipedia.org/wiki/Mule_deer. Retrieved on 10 February 2019

Wikipedia. (2019). North American River Otter: en.wikipedia.org/wiki/North_American_River_Otter. Retrieved on 10 February 2019

Wikipedia. (2019). Opossum: en.wikipedia.org/wiki/opossum. Retrieved on 23 August 2019

Wikipedia. (2019). Pika: en.wikipedia.org/wiki/Pika. Retrieved on 10 February 2019

Wikipedia. (2019). Porcupine: en.wikipedia.org/wiki/ Porcupine. Retrieved on 10 February 2019

Wikipedia. (2019). Prairie dog: en.wikipedia.org/wiki/ Prairie_dog. Retrieved on 20 February 2019

Wikipedia. (2019). Raccoon: en.wikipedia.org/wiki/ Raccoon. Retrieved on 23 August 2019

Wikipedia. (2019). Red Fox: en.wikipedia.org/wiki/ Red_fox. Retrieved on 20 February 2019

Wikipedia. (2019). Reindeer: en.wikipedia.org/wiki/ Reindeer. Retrieved on 23 August 2019

Wikipedia. (2019). Ruffed Grouse: en.wikipedia.org/ wiki/Ruffed_grouse. Retrieved on 10 February 2019

Wikipedia. (2019). Snowshoe Hare: en.wikipedia.org/ wiki/Snowshoe_hare. Retrieved on 10 February 2019

Wikipedia. (2019). Striped Skunk: en.wikipedia.org/ wiki/Striped_skunk. Retrieved on 15 September 2019

Wikipedia. (2019). Western toad: en.wikipedia.org/ wiki/Western_toad. Retrieved on 23 August 2019

Wikipedia. (2019). White Tailed Deer: en.wikipedia. org/wiki/White_tailed_deer. Retrieved on 10 February 2019

Wikipedia. (2019). Wild turkey: en.wikipedia.org/ wiki/Wild_turkey. Retrieved on 23 August 2019

Wikipedia. (2019). Wolf: en.wikipedia.org/wiki/wolf. Retrieved on 17 February 2019

Wikihow & Pawlisch, D. (2019). How to Catch a Bullfrog. Wikihow: www.wikihow.com/catch-a-bullfrog#. Retrieved on 16 September 2019

Wood, W.F., Sollers, B.G., Dragoo, G.A. et al. (2002). Volatile Components in Defensive Spray of the Hooded Skunk, Mephitis macroura. Journal of Chemical Ecology 28, 1865–1870. https://doi. org/10.1023/A:1020573404341

World Wildlife Fund. (2020) Eight Surprising Prairie Dog Facts. Worldwildlife.org/stories/8-surprising-prairie-dog-facts. Downloaded 11 April 2020

CPSIA information can be obtained
at www.ICGtesting.com
Printed in the USA
FSHW011152211020
74928FS